——— LOST ———
CHESTER RIVER
STEAMBOATS

LOST
CHESTER RIVER
STEAMBOATS

FROM CHESTERTOWN TO BALTIMORE

JACK SHAUM

THE
History
PRESS

Published by The History Press
Charleston, SC
www.historypress.net

Front cover: The steamer *B.S. Ford* leaving Chestertown. *Postcard from the author's collection.*
Back cover, top: Steamer *Emma A. Ford*. *Courtesy Chesapeake Bay Maritime Museum, H. Graham Wood Collection*; *bottom*: Steamer landing at Rock Hall, Maryland. *Postcard from the author's collection.*

First published 2015

Manufactured in the United States

ISBN 978.1.46711.759.3

Library of Congress Control Number: 2015947033

To Martha—wife, soulmate and best friend

CONTENTS

ACKNOWLEDGEMENTS

A work of history represents the efforts of many people, and I am extremely grateful to all those who inspired me and assisted me in telling the story of steamboats on the Chester River. I must begin with the two men who first opened my eyes to the wonders of traveling the Chesapeake's rivers by steamboat. The late H. Graham Wood and the late Robert H. Burgess were friends from my late teens onward and allowed me access to their wide-ranging knowledge of steamboat information. Their 1968 book, *Steamboats Out of Baltimore*, is the definitive source of information on Bay steamers. It covers every steamboat line that operated from Baltimore from 1813 until 1962 and provided many leads in creating this book. The late David C. Holly, another good friend, created three outstanding books on Chesapeake Bay steamers, and these, too, proved to be great sources of information. His book *Exodus 1947* is simply the best account of a Chesapeake Bay steamboat that became one of history's most famous refugee ships.

A number of institutions opened their files and provided not only information but also photographs and ships' plans. Lynne Phillips at the Chesapeake Bay Maritime Museum made available the hundreds of photographs that Graham Wood bequeathed to the museum, along with multiple copies of *Merchant Vessels of the United States*. Lynne was persistent in her efforts to ensure that the best possible image reproductions could be had. Claudia Jew at the Mariners' Museum went the extra mile in searching for images of Chester River steamers, having them scanned and offering advice. One of her major finds in the museum archives was plans to the steamers *B.S. Ford*, *Emma A. Ford* and *Corsica*, which likely went untouched for decades. At the Maryland Historical Society, Debbie Harner made me feel right at home and supplied files and photos pertaining to the Chester River boats. Eben Dennis at the Enoch Pratt Free Library's Maryland Department patiently helped me navigate its extensive collection, which proved to be a gold mine. Chris Baer at the Hagley Museum opened up the museum's collection of Pennsylvania Railroad records, which included minutes of the Chester River Steamboat Company directors and annual reports of the Maryland, Delaware and Virginia Railway. Justin Demski at the Maryland State Archives provided a fine photograph of the Chester River Steamboat Company dock in Baltimore.

Closer to home, I was provided access to the archives of the Historical Society of Kent County by archivist Joan Andersen and was given many helpful suggestions and advice by the society's Steve Frohock and executive director Karen Emerson. The archives of the Queen Anne's County Historical Society were made available by society vice-president Rebecca Marquardt, and society past president Scott MacGlashan offered much encouragement and suggested additional resources. Jack Broderick and the Kent Island Heritage Society came up with a number of very useful leads. David Fike, president of APG Chesapeake, which owns the *Record Observer*, *Kent County News* and *Bay Times* in Queen Anne's County, graciously gave permission to reproduce steamboat advertisements from the nineteenth-century predecessors of those publications. Editors Angela Price and Dan Divilio helped gain access to old newspapers.

Steamboat historian and friend extraordinaire Bill Ewen of Providence, Rhode Island, searched his extensive collection and came up with some outstanding illustrations of Chester River steamers that apparently are not available in this neck of the woods. Mark Newsome of Chestertown has an unmatched collection of memorabilia and paper ephemera on Kent and Queen Anne's Counties, and his postcard collection alone yielded some interesting new (to me, anyway) images, as well as the first Chester River Steamboat Company pass that I have ever laid eyes on. Bruce Burgess, son of Robert H. Burgess, located a photograph from his father's collection of the steamer *B.S. Ford* in its final role as a barge. A photograph of the Indiantown Wharf piled high with peaches and tomatoes was loaned by Mary Wood, whose evocative book, *My Darling Alice*, takes us back to those days of living along the river when steamboat visits were commonplace. I was amazed to find that the restored Indiantown Wharf still exists in its original configuration—said to be the only one on the river—and I was given a tour of it by Robin Wood and Mary and Howard McCoy, who live on Indiantown Farm just a stone's throw from the wharf. Melissa Baile of the Friends of Eastern Neck and Cindy Beemiller of the U.S. Fish and Wildlife Service allowed me to see the service's archives on Eastern Neck Island, once an important freight port of the Chester River steamers. Longtime friend and historian Ralph Eshelman provided information on British efforts to capture the *Chesapeake* during the War of 1812.

A hearty thank-you goes to Kevin Hemstock, author of *Injustice on the Eastern Shore: Race and the Hill Murder Trial*, published earlier in 2015, for introducing me to his publisher, The History Press. Kevin was also a tremendous source of information, accumulated over more than a decade of research and collecting. His advice on historical matters and the technical aspects of writing a book on local history were invaluable to me. Both Kevin and Steve Frohock of the Historical Society of Kent County read the manuscript, clarifying certain items and offering a host of useful suggestions.

At The History Press, editor Hannah Cassilly cheerfully guided me through the digital publishing process and provided encouragement and advice. The publishing industry has changed quite a bit since my first book, *Majesty at Sea*, was published thirty-four years ago, and I cannot thank Hannah enough for everything she did. An unexpected aside was to learn that we have mutual connections here in Maryland.

I thank my wife, Martha, for reading and rereading chapters and recommending refinements, encouraging me every step of the way, tolerating my reaction to computer snafus and being there for me, as she has been for the past forty-three years.

A final word of appreciation goes to our beloved Australian shepherd, Annie, who sat under my table or next to me every step of the way while I was working. There is something about the devotion and calming influence of a faithful dog.

Without the assistance of everyone named above, the work very well may have been stillborn. My unbounded thanks go out to all.

INTRODUCTION

When I was eight years old, my parents took me on an overnight trip down Chesapeake Bay from Baltimore to Norfolk on the venerable steamboat *City of Richmond* of the Old Bay Line. It was only a twelve-hour voyage, but for me, it might as well have been a transatlantic crossing on the *Queen Mary.* I was mesmerized about everything as I walked through the corridors of that 1913 vintage steamer—the polished interior woodwork, the brass facing on the main staircase, the stained-glass domes over the main saloon (yes, that's what it was called), the gentle pulsing of the engine far below, the rich tones of the steam whistle as it echoed across the water.

Before that night was over, I was totally hooked. My mother knew Captain Samuel B. Chapman, the steamer's master, and that allowed us the opportunity to visit places usually off-limits to passengers—the engine room and the pilothouse—and to sit down for a visit in the captain's cabin, the walls of which were covered with memorabilia of various Chesapeake Bay steamboats. The real magic occurred after dark, when Captain Chapman took me into the darkened pilothouse with its gleaming brass equipment and a great wooden wheel that was even taller than I was. Before reluctantly leaving to go to bed, I had the opportunity to take the wheel and read the radar. The next morning on arrival in Norfolk, the captain let me blow the whistle as we approached the dock. How could an eight-year-old not be captivated by such an experience?

While my first interest in Chesapeake Bay steamboats was the big night boats between Baltimore and Norfolk, I have also long appreciated the smaller vessels that steamed up the Chesapeake's many tributaries and have been researching them for many years. Living near the Chester River, I became especially interested in the steamboats that ran up and down the river for over one hundred years. Very little has been published about these steamers, and I decided that it was time to tell their stories.

In their time, the steamboats were as important to residents of the Eastern Shore as their cars are today. Overland travel to the Western Shore for personal reasons or on business was difficult at best, and the steamers offered a regularly scheduled, reliable and pleasant way to avoid that. They were essential to the farmers who grew crops and raised livestock and needed to quickly get their products to market in Baltimore. On returning to the Eastern Shore, the boats would bring things not readily available in the rural areas then—manufactured goods, medicine, building materials and fertilizer. Many shore residents took the boat to Baltimore to buy clothes, shop in the big department stores, go to medical appointments and visit relatives. Simply put, the steamboat was extremely important to the local economy and to the way of life of many shore families.

Sadly, the steamboat seems to have been all but forgotten today. The boats themselves are long gone, there are few tangible reminders and virtually no historical markers commemorate their contribution to the growth of Maryland. The emphasis in recent decades has been on our maritime sailing heritage, a movement that has succeeded admirably in drawing attention to sailing ships, historic and otherwise.

But shouldn't the steamboat get equal time?

Hopefully, this book will help fill that void.

1.

WHEN THE BAY REGION'S HIGHWAYS WERE MADE OF WATER

No one knows for sure why Captain John Smith bypassed the Chester River on his second voyage around the Chesapeake Bay in the summer of 1608, but he missed a good bet. It is known that he explored the Sassafras River to the north and interacted with the Indians there and that he appears to have stopped near present-day Rock Hall, Maryland; however, he then continued on to the Western Shore of the Bay and returned to Jamestown, Virginia. One theory is that as he sailed south along the western coastline of Maryland's Eastern Shore, he mistook the wide mouth of the Chester for a large cove or perhaps a huge sound, such as Tangier or Pocomoke farther down the Bay.

Having been taken by his experiences with the Tockwogh Indians along the banks of the Sassafras, the noted explorer would likely have been equally taken with the Chester—a longer, wider and deeper river coursing through a verdant countryside where he would most likely have met up with other Indians. While the Tockwogh inhabited the Sassafras shoreline, it is believed that the Ozinies lived along the Chester and that there might also have been Monoponson people living on Kent Island and around the mouth of the river. One wonders what discoveries Smith could have added to his findings had he sailed up the Chester.[1]

The Chester, named for the city of Chester in England, is one of the longest rivers on the Eastern Shore and begins near the present-day town of Millington, Maryland, which straddles the line between Kent and Queen Anne's Counties. It is formed by the confluence of the Cypress Branch and

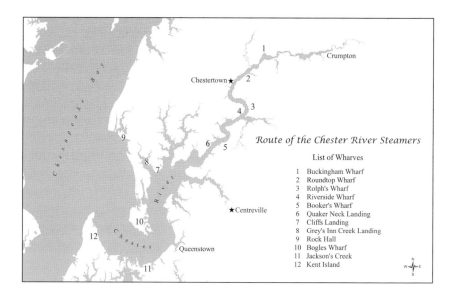

The Chester River is navigable for approximately thirty-two miles from Crumpton to its mouth. Here are the locations of some of the steamer wharves. *Courtesy of J. Herring.*

the Andover Branch, both of which originate in Delaware. The river is about forty-three miles long and ranges in width from half a mile to three miles at its mouth, north of Kent Island. It is quite deep in some places, the channel reaching a depth of fifty-six feet in some places. The shoreline of the Chester River today is probably much the same as it was in colonial times and remains largely undeveloped. "After the Choptank, the Chester is the noblest of Eastern Shore rivers," wrote Hulbert Footner in his celebrated *Rivers of the Eastern Shore.*[2] The Choptank is another major river farther south on the Eastern Shore.

Land grants to European settlers along the Chester were first made in the 1650s, first in the area near Queenstown where Lord Baltimore granted Henry DeCoursey as much land as his thumb could cover on a map. It was known as My Lord's Gift. Later, Chestertown became the Kent County seat, and nearly a century after that, the Queen Anne's County seat was moved from Queenstown to Centreville.

Very early on, the Chester proved to be a particularly lucrative maritime highway linking the rural Eastern Shore with the Western Shore and Baltimore in particular. It proved to be more expedient to go by water rather than endure the grueling stagecoach ride up the Eastern Shore, around the top of the Bay and down the other side. The roads were primitive by almost any definition and ranged from dusty and bumpy to wet and muddy depending on the season. No matter the condition of the roads, the trip could be a long and difficult one. Railroads were still several decades in the future.

The towns of Chestertown, Queenstown, Centreville and Crumpton developed along the banks of the river and its tributaries in the late seventeenth and early eighteenth centuries, along with many large farms and plantations that over time had their own wharves from which to ship and receive goods. Names like Buckingham Wharf, Roundtop Wharf, Rolph's Wharf, Quaker Neck Landing, Indiantown and Grey's Inn Creek identified those wharves in the early years, and in many cases, those names are still used to describe specific locales. Farms along the river initially produced tobacco and then went over to grains; corn; a variety of vegetables and fruits, particularly peaches; and livestock. Just before the turn of the twentieth century, the area along the upper reaches of the Chester was known as one of the world's largest peach-producing regions, and the steamboats carried millions of those peaches to market. Watermen working the river caught a wide variety of fish, crabs and oysters, which, along with the farm products, had to get to market, and that's where the river came in. It became home to a waterborne transportation system that lasted for nearly a century and a quarter and initially included sailing vessels, followed by steamboats. While these vessels took Eastern Shore farm products and seafood to market in Baltimore, they also carried passengers down the river and across the Bay for trips to the city to shop or visit relatives. On the return trip to the shore, they brought manufactured goods from the city to the rural areas—everything from dresses and shoes to tools, farm implements and medicines. In addition, the U.S. mail was an important customer of the steamers over the years. For decades, numerous vessels could be seen moving up and down the Chester on a daily basis, all year long.

Many of the early sailing vessels, called packets, running between Chester River points and Baltimore were independently owned—that is, they were not operated by a specific shipping company. It appears that one of the first scheduled sailing packets was the *Two Brothers*, which began operations in June 1803 between Baltimore and Chestertown. She was owned by Captain John Allen and captained by Joseph Garnett.[3] Even though travel by water was infinitely better than by land, sailing vessels were at the mercy of the wind, which could, and often did, slow them down. One particularly difficult stretch was the portion of the river known as Devil's Reach between

Chestertown and Rolph's Wharf, where the river twists from a southwesterly direction to southeasterly, complicating the passage of a sailing ship. Besides the wind issues in that section of the river, there were also shoals to be avoided, a problem that present-day boaters say still exists. Other sailing vessels known to have operated between the Chester River and Baltimore in the first two decades of the nineteenth century were the *Independence* and the *General LaFayette*. One of those schooners—the *Thomas Jefferson*, also referred to as the Queenstown Packet because of her regular route between that town and Baltimore—ran afoul of the British fleet that was marauding Chesapeake Bay in 1813 and 1814. On April 16, 1813, she was boarded outside Baltimore by British sailors, towed to the British squadron and put into service for the Royal Navy. Ultimately, however, her passengers and cargo were released.

Steamboats made their first appearance in the waning years of the eighteenth century and began to come into their own early in the second decade of the nineteenth as they became more reliable. A Dorchester County seafarer named Edward Trippe is the man most often credited with bringing the steamboat to the Chesapeake.[4] He was the driving force behind the construction of the *Chesapeake*, the first steamboat to navigate her namesake waters. The *Chesapeake* was a side-wheel steamer built in Baltimore in 1813. She had a wooden hull 130 feet long with a beam (width) of 22 feet and a mast on which could be rigged a sail to help her along or in the event of engine failure. She burned pine logs for fuel. Accommodations below deck were somewhat Spartan but included a ladies' cabin; a gentlemen's cabin, where meals were served; and rudimentary sleeping accommodations. The *Chesapeake* made her maiden voyage from Baltimore to Annapolis on June 13, 1813, and then made a trip across the Bay to Rock Hall a week later—apparently the very first steamboat to journey to the Eastern Shore.[5] After that, she settled down on a regular run between Baltimore and Frenchtown at the head of the Bay, where passengers connected with a coach that took them to the Delaware River, where they boarded another boat to complete their journey to Philadelphia.

Although the *Chesapeake* made her debut at the same time that British warships were prowling the Bay during the War of 1812, she never came into contact with one, but it wasn't because the British weren't trying. On July 11, 1814, Rear Admiral George Cockburn told his colleagues that he wanted to "get hold of the Steam Boat" and instructed that efforts be made in the upper Chesapeake to find and take the *Chesapeake*. But on July 18, he wrote to Admiral Alexander Cochrane, "I am sorry to report that [HMS

Loire] missed the Steam Boat by a few hours only."[6] There does not appear to be any further mention of the steamboat playing a part in the British plans a little less than two months before the Battle of Baltimore.

Initially, the run between Baltimore and Frenchtown was the primary steamboat route on the Bay, but with time, steamers took up others, including the long trip down the Bay to Norfolk and to various rivers on the Eastern and Western Shores, such as the Choptank, Nanticoke, Piankatank and Patuxent. As it turned out, the first regularly scheduled steamboat service from Baltimore to the Eastern Shore was to the Chester River beginning on April 1, 1821, when the steamer *Maryland* began operating to Queenstown and Chestertown.[7]

Like so many of the early steamers, the *Maryland* was run by an independent owner not affiliated with any formal company. Built in 1818, she was 137 feet long with a beam of 26 feet and a draft (the depth to which the vessel sits in the water) of just under 5 feet. "The *Maryland* is one of the most beautiful boats of Baltimore," declared Jean Baptiste Marestier, a French engineer who came to the United States to study the many steamboats that were starting to populate East Coast waterways. "There are two cylindrical boilers, one on each side of the engine," he wrote. "This arrangement leaves plenty of living space but it is only possible when boats are very broad. There are no berths except in the forward cabin."[8] The observant Frenchman kept copious notes and determined that the *Maryland*'s engine produced about sixty horsepower and that her 19-foot-diameter paddle wheels made seventeen to eighteen revolutions a minute, which translated to a speed of about seven knots, making it possible for her to easily cross from Baltimore to Chestertown in less than one day.

By way of contrast, J. Thomas Scharf, in his monumental *History of Baltimore City and County*, stated, "The accommodations of the *Maryland* were of a very primitive and limited description, the hull being occupied by the engine and boilers, but also for the storage of freight and cord-wood, then used exclusively to make steam."[9]

The steamboat's schedule called for departure from Baltimore's Market Street wharf at 5:00 a.m. on Monday mornings headed for Chestertown with a stop at Queenstown and arrival at the Kent County seat around noon. The trip cost $1.50 each way. The *Maryland* then laid over for the night at the foot of High Street in Chestertown and returned to Baltimore on Tuesday. It was a route that the boat would continue to operate for more than twenty years. During this early period, she also made regular trips from Baltimore to Easton. Her master at the time was Captain Clement

Scenes along the Chester River are largely unchanged from those in the nineteenth century. The stakes in the foreground are for pound nets. *Author's photograph.*

Vickers.[10] Within a few years, the *Maryland* was also operating between Baltimore and the Corsica River, probably stopping at Earles and Puseys, two landings along that small river.

Another very early steamer on the Chester River was the *Surprise*, which operated between Baltimore and Centreville on the Corsica River, a tributary of the Chester above Queenstown. The precise date of her debut on the river is unclear since several sources disagree on when she first operated there. At ninety-four feet long with a beam of fifteen and a half feet and a draft of four feet, she was smaller than the *Maryland*. Built in 1816, she operated on a number of Chesapeake Bay routes in addition to making runs to and from Centreville.[11] As on other early steamers, the helmsman operated a tiller rather than a wheel, and the captain sent messages to the engine room below his place on deck by a system of foot stamping on the wooden deck. The *Surprise*'s first master on its Chester River trips was Captain Jonathan Spencer. There are also accounts of the steamer *Patuxent* competing for a short time with the *Maryland* on the Baltimore–Chestertown route.

Shippers and passengers alike welcomed the new method of transportation, which, over the long haul, proved to be extremely reliable and largely accident free.

The steamboat had come to the Chester River to stay.

2.

INDEPENDENT OPERATORS ON THE CHESTER RIVER

Once the steamboat had its foot in the door of the Chester River trade, it seemed as if everyone wanted to get a piece of the action. Independently operated steamboats began to materialize—not only on the Chester but also on other rivers on both the Eastern and Western Shores. Within a short time, there were steamers operating between Baltimore and points on the Choptank, Sassafras, Susquehanna, Miles and Nanticoke Rivers, to name just a few. And it was not uncommon to see a specific steamer operate one or two days a week to one river and then one or two days in the same week to another. One almost needed a scorecard to keep track of which vessel was operating where and when.

It appears that the *Maryland* pretty much had the Chester to herself in the early going. Except for occasional trips by the 1817-built *Surprise*, the *Maryland* was alone most of the time on the Chester between 1820 and 1827. She was running between Baltimore and Chestertown, and we know that she called at Queenstown; however, it is not clear what country wharves she might have also visited.[12] After 1827, the steamer *Patuxent*, which was built that year, ran opposite the *Maryland* for a short time, but she spent most of her career elsewhere.

To give some idea of how the steamers were shifted from route to route, the *Maryland*, in addition to Chester River runs, also ran a few days each week from Baltimore to Annapolis and landings along the Choptank River, as well as occasionally to Rappahannock River points in Virginia. At the same time, the *Patuxent* was making a number of trips to the Sassafras River from Baltimore, to the Wicomico River on the lower Eastern Shore and to the Patuxent and Rappahannock Rivers on the western shores of both Maryland and Virginia. In those early days, there was no daily service.

While so many of the other river runs were overnight trips, the Chester River voyages were done in daylight and usually required up to eight hours to complete. That could vary depending on how many wharves the steamers called on and how much time they spent loading and unloading at each. At the end of the trip in either Chestertown or Baltimore, the vessel and her crew spent the night in port before heading out on the return trip early the next morning.

These early steamboat operations were usually the work of a single man or a man and several partners who had purchased a vessel but without having formed a company. That is why so many of the early advertisements for the river steamers prominently featured the name of the vessel, rather than that of a company. The identity of the owners could be found at the bottom of an advertisement, in such designations as Wm. Owen, agent, or S.M. Shoemaker, agent. In some cases, these owners/agents were also captains or pursers of the steamers and remained on the scene for many years, owning and operating many different vessels.

These early steamers were rather modest vessels by today's standards but huge by the standards of the second and third decades of the nineteenth century. All were built of wood and propelled by side wheels. They were in the neighborhood of 135 feet in length with beams of 20 to 25 feet, not including the enormous paddle wheels. Their gross tonnage (the measurement of enclosed space rather than weight) was on the order of 200 to 290 gross tons. The steam engines of the time burned wood, and as mentioned earlier, the vessels carried auxiliary sails to assist the engine or provide propulsion in the event the engine failed en route. They could do about seven or so miles an hour. For some reason, the speed of Chesapeake Bay steamers was always measured in miles an hour rather than knots, as on oceangoing ships.

In 1830, the *Maryland*, commanded at that time by Captain Lemuel G. Taylor, altered her schedule somewhat by departing Baltimore on Mondays at 7:00 a.m. for Centreville on the Corsica River and then Chestertown. At the same time, a new vessel appeared on the scene. She was the *Gov. Wolcott*, named for Roger Wolcott, governor of Connecticut in pre-Revolutionary days. She was built in 1825 for service around New York and then brought to Maryland to run between Baltimore, Havre de Grace and Port Deposit on the upper Western Shore and Georgetown and Fredericktown on the Sassafras on the upper Eastern Shore. She also sailed between Baltimore, Rock Hall and Chestertown in 1830 and for several years thereafter:

> *The Steam Boat* Gov. Wolcott, *Capt. Verdon, will continue to leave Baltimore every Thursday morning at 9 o'clock, stop at Rockhall* [sic] *at 12 noon and at Corsica wharf at about 3 P.M. and at Chestertown at 5 P.M. Returning—will leave Chestertown at 8 o'clock on Friday morning, Corsica at 10 and Rockhall at about 1 P.M., and arrive at Baltimore at 4 P.M. Wm. Owen agent. Passage from Balt. To Rockhall $1,25* [sic] [and] *Corsica 2. Chestertown 2. All Bagages* [sic] *at the risk of the owners thereof.*[13]

From 1830 through 1843, these two steamers, operated by different owners and the only ones on the run, competed with each other on the Chester River trade. For a brief period around 1836, the steamer *Norfolk* appeared on the Chester River route, running between Baltimore, Corsica and Queenstown, under the command of Captain Joseph Pearson. She had been built in 1817 for the Baltimore to Richmond service and later operated from Baltimore to Havre de Grace and Port Deposit on the Susquehanna River, in addition to her short stint on the Chester River.

Although the steamboat was rapidly cornering the market on trips between Chester River ports and Baltimore, the sailing packets were still part of the equation. The schooner *Two Brothers* is known to have still been on the route between Centreville and Baltimore in 1832, when she was promoted as an elegant and fast vessel that carried freight and passengers "on liberal terms."[14] She left Centreville every Wednesday at 9:00 a.m. and left Baltimore for the return voyage at 9:00 a.m. on Saturday. The length of the trip depended on how the wind was blowing. Her season began in June and likely lasted through the fall until winter weather closed in. Her owners, Augustus McCabe and William Henry Wilmer, stated in advertising copy that she would be able to "give general satisfaction, and hope to at least share a portion of public patronage."[15] They also promised to carefully handle grain and other commodities and provide comfortable accommodations for passengers. A postscript to a newspaper advertisement stated that the mailbag from the *Two Brothers* would be left at John R. Driver's store in Centreville. The sailing vessels continued to hang on, and as late as August 1841, the sloop *George Washington* was making a run between Chestertown and Annapolis, apparently the only vessel to operate on such an itinerary. In fact, some commercial sailing vessels (other than oyster boats and the like) were seen on the Chesapeake Bay well into the twentieth century. Large deep-sea freight-carrying schooners continued to operate on the Bay and Atlantic Ocean until the late 1930s in some cases.

In those days, it would not have been uncommon for some of the vessels to stop operating in the winter months and go into seasonal layup. They would usually return to service in the early spring, as evidenced by an announcement on March 23, 1840, that the *Gov. Wolcott* would resume her runs within a few days. It was noted that the steamer had been lengthened during the off-season, that her hull and engines had undergone major overhauls and that she was in top condition to start a new season. Her schedule at that time called for a departure from Patterson's Wharf in Baltimore every Thursday morning at 9:00 a.m. with calls at Rock Hall, Corsica and Chestertown. She returned on Friday and, on other days of the week, ran from Baltimore to Port Deposit and Havre de Grace, both on the Susquehanna River.

Another competitor appeared in May 1841, when the steamer *Chesapeake*, operated by the aforementioned S.M. Shoemaker, came on the route. The *Chesapeake* (not to be confused with the Bay's pioneer steamboat of 1813) was built in 1834 in Washington, D.C., and was 234 gross tons, which made her a little smaller than the *Maryland* but larger than the *Gov. Wolcott.* She also departed Baltimore on Thursday mornings, returning from Chestertown the next day. Like the other steamers, she made runs at least once a week from Baltimore to Port Deposit. The *Chesapeake* apparently did not last long on the Chester, for she disappears from the record soon after, although she lasted somewhere until being abandoned in 1854.

June 1841 saw the *Maryland* embark on a schedule that had her making the round trip between Baltimore, Centreville and Chestertown in one day, apparently the first time such a journey had been done. She left Dugan's Wharf near what is now Baltimore's Inner Harbor at 6:00 a.m., calling at both towns, and returned around sunset. A ticket to Centreville or Chestertown was $2.50. The next month, a new steamer appeared on the river. She was the *Boston* and had been built in 1831 for service between New York and Boston, though later she traveled between New York and Providence, Rhode Island. Described in contemporary advertisements as a "large and commodious steamboat," she also made the round trip in one day, about which Captain Kenney, her operator, said, "to families and others, this offers a favourable opportunity."[16]

Unfortunately, photographs of these early steamboats do not seem to exist, so it is difficult to tell how one differed from another in appearance. One certainly could not judge from the steamboat images that appeared in many of the advertisements of the day because the same generic steamer was used for all of them.

When the boats were not on their regularly scheduled runs, they were often busy taking passengers on excursions. One such early pleasure trip was made by the *Boston* on July 23, 1841, when she brought excursionists to Chestertown from Baltimore. Having left Baltimore early that morning, she arrived in Chestertown around noon with about three hundred people aboard, including a military band that played during the crossing and as she docked at the foot of High Street. It was apparently a typical July day with temperatures over ninety degrees when she departed at 4:00 p.m., but the *Kent News* noted that "the wind being from the South, and a bit fresh, the return trip, we hope, was a pleasant one."[17]

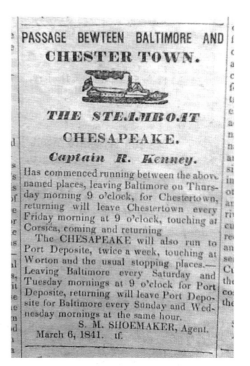

PASSAGE BEWTEEN BALTIMORE AND CHESTER TOWN.

THE STEAMBOAT CHESAPEAKE. Captain R. Kenney.

Has commenced running between the above named places, leaving Baltimore on Thursday morning 9 o'clock, for Chestertown, returning will leave Chestertown every Friday morning at 9 o'clock, touching at Corsica, coming and returning

The CHESAPEAKE will also run to Port Deposite, twice a week, touching at Worton and the usual stopping places.— Leaving Baltimore every Saturday and Tuesday mornings at 9 o'clock for Port Deposite, returning will leave Port Deposite for Baltimore every Sunday and Wednesday mornings at the same hour.

S. M. SHOEMAKER, Agent.
March 6, 1841. tf.

The independent steamer *Chesapeake* was advertised in March 1841 as making one round trip a week between Chestertown and Baltimore. *From the* Kent News.

Word circulated in Chestertown in the early fall of 1841 that an effort was underway to enlist subscribers to help with the purchase of a steamer to be built specifically with the Chester River route in mind. The shares reportedly were going for twenty-five dollars each; however, little else was heard of the plan, and a new boat was not built.

In 1843, the steamer *Osiris* appeared on the route, sailing from Baltimore's Inner Harbor on Wednesdays at 7:00 a.m. for Centreville and Chestertown. Built in New York in 1838, she was about the same size as the *Gov. Wolcott*, which had left the run earlier that year. The *Osiris*, which would eventually come under control of the Confederate States of America during the Civil War, remained in competition with the *Maryland* for about three years and also made the round trip in a single day. The service, at this point, was still one or two times a week, with the boats off on other runs other days of the

In this rare Baltimore Harbor photograph, the *Osiris* is seen at the left, tied up alongside the *Herald* of the Baltimore Steam Packet Company. *Courtesy Chesapeake Bay Maritime Museum, H. Graham Wood Collection.*

week. In the case of the *Osiris*, she ran on those other days from Baltimore to Annapolis and points on the Choptank River, including Cambridge, Dover Bridge and Denton, laying over for the night and returning to Baltimore the next day.

Another steamer, the *Fredericksburg*, also operated by S.M. Shoemaker, arrived on the route in February 1842, and she was given a big buildup in advertising copy that preceded her arrival:

> *The* Fredericksburg *has been recently overhaulded* [sic], *and put in complete order, is well adapted to the carrying of freight and passengers, is commanded by experience* [sic] *officers, and no exertion will be spared to give satisfaction…She will* [sic] *also furnished with bags sufficient to carry any quantity of grain that may offer.*[18]

The *Fredericksburg* began the season with one trip a week, and it was stated that if she proved popular, a second trip would be offered each week. Later in the 1842 season, she also made trips from Baltimore to Fredericktown on the Sassafras River and landings on Worton Creek in Kent County. She was under the command of Captain John B. Gray and was based at Baltimore's Light Street docks, which were already becoming the heart of steamboat operations on the Bay and its rivers. Dozens of steamers could be tied up at the docks on any given day while an equal number were out on their runs. Although the *Fredericksburg* was on the Chester River run in 1842, she disappears from the route's shipping rolls after that season.

A sign of the times manifested itself in a special trip made by the *Maryland* on September 12, 1842, that was labeled the Grand Temperance Excursion from Baltimore to Chestertown and return in one day. "Those wishing to have a pleasant trip to the Eastern Shore will have a favorable opportunity,"[19] stated the advertisement promoting the excursion. (Some might read between the lines and conclude that perhaps some of the non-temperance cruises were less than favorable!) Advertisements specified no alcoholic beverages, dinner on board for twenty-five cents and "ice cream and confectionary for the accommodation of ladies."[20]

There's some uncertainty about what happened next to the *Maryland*. H. Graham Wood and Robert H. Burgess, two historians who are widely respected as the most knowledgeable experts on Chesapeake Bay steamers, suggested in 1968 that she remained on the Chester River until 1846.[21] However, writing in the 1880s, when memories might have been fresh on such matters, Queen Anne's County historian Frederic Emory reported that she was replaced in 1844 by the steamer *Thomas Jefferson*, having been purchased by Captain Taylor, who, in addition to being the *Maryland*'s skipper, was also her owner.[22] It is known that in 1845, the *Maryland* was making occasional excursions to Worton Creek in Kent County. Built in 1834, the *Jefferson* had operated on just about every Chesapeake Bay itinerary, including a run from Norfolk to Richmond, before being bought for Chester River service. She apparently did not remain on the Chester for very long, for there is very little mention of her after the initial report of her purchase.

Travel by steamboat continued to grow in popularity through the 1840s and early 1850s and saw a number of vessels come and go. The service between Baltimore and Chester River points, however, still was not daily, as many of the vessels ran to other rivers on other days of the week. In 1850, there were two boats making three departures a week from Baltimore for the Chester. The *Hugh Jenkins* was a nearly new vessel of 306 tons built in Baltimore in 1849 that left the city at 7:00 a.m. on Wednesdays and Saturdays making calls in both directions at Kent Island near the mouth of the Chester River. That appears to have been the first time steamers stopped at Kent Island. On Thursday mornings, the 462-ton *Cambridge* of

1846 would leave her Light Street wharf for points along the Chester, also calling at Kent Island. The increase in the number of trips each week proved popular among Eastern Shore merchants doing business with companies in Baltimore.

The *Osiris* returned to the route in 1851 and was paired with the *Hugh Jenkins* after the *Cambridge* moved on elsewhere after a relatively brief time on the river. Other steamers finding the Chester River run to be lucrative included the *Cecil* and the *William Selden*, which operated on the route in 1852 and early 1853. The *William Selden*, built in Washington in 1852, was described as "new and splendid"[23] and was under the command of Captain J.D. Turner. She also touched at Kent Island, as did the *Osiris*, which continued beyond Chestertown in 1852 to call at Crumpton, near the head of navigation. This might have been among the earliest instances of a steamboat visiting at the town.

A company named the Eastern Shore Steamboat Company was formed around 1850 to operate steamers from Baltimore to a number of rivers. This firm is different from the one that formed in 1867 and operated until

The *Hugh Jenkins* first operated on the Chester River in 1853. It was acquired by the Federal government for service in the Civil War. *The Mariners' Museum, Newport News, Virginia.*

1894. It was managing the *Hugh Jenkins* and *Osiris* as of October 1853, with the *Jenkins* sailing Monday mornings from Baltimore for Chestertown with stops in Queenstown and the regular wharves along the river—Booker's, Quaker Neck and Rolph's. Her master, at that time, was Captain James Tilghman, a local favorite. The *Osiris*, under command of Captain John H. Kirwan, departed Baltimore every Wednesday morning and made stops at Kent Island, Grey's Inn Creek, Queenstown, Corsica, Harrison's and Chestertown. This was likely the earliest instance of steamers visiting Grey's Inn Creek, a tributary of the Chester between Eastern Neck Island and the Kent County mainland. Both steamers made round trips in a single day.

The name of the Eastern Shore Steamboat Company fades from view in the mid-1850s at about the same time that another independent steamer, the *Georgia*, built in 1836, made some trips on the Chester under charter. The year 1857 saw a nearly new steamer begin operations on the river, a vessel that was to remain for many years. She was the *Arrow*, and she was owned and operated by a man who was to leave a permanent mark in the history of steamboats on the Chester River.

His name was Henry B. Slaughter.

ENTER THE SLAUGHTER LINE

Henry B. Slaughter was originally from Delaware, but he became best known along the Chester River and all the way to Baltimore through his founding of a major steamboat company. Born on October 29, 1817, he was one of seven children and made his way early in life as a farmer. He moved to Maryland about 1843 and established his farm in the vicinity of Crumpton. When he arrived in Maryland, he apparently did so without a lot of money and bought farm property that was described as nearly barren. His arrival reportedly went largely unnoticed, but it didn't take long for him to make his mark in the local business community through his farming. He devoted much time to studying methods of preserving peaches and other goods and eventually came up with a system of preserving fruits, meats and vegetables in cans or jars that were hermetically sealed. He was granted a patent on his new process on November 11, 1862, by which time he had been in the steamboat business for several years.

In 1846, Slaughter bought an eighteenth-century home on the Kent County side of the Chester River across from Crumpton known as either Townside or Comegys House and began to expand his farming operations. Soon after, he built a sawmill, a cannery, tenant houses and a large barn on the property. Townside was to have been the name of a community planned on the Kent County side of the river in that area, but it failed to flourish.[24] The property remained in the Slaughter family until it was sold at auction in 1874. The house still stands.

"By his bold and enterprising mind and habits of industry he has given to this locality a reputation for business and thrift far in advance of any other in this or the adjoining counties," the *Kent News* noted of him at the time of his death in 1865. "Mr. Slaughter was emphatically a man of progress, fully up to the present age."[25] As his farming and canning operations flourished, he knew that he would need a reliable method of transportation to get his peaches, fruits and other products to market in Baltimore, and that's what led to the creation of what became known as the "Daily Line" or "Slaughter's Line for the Chester River."

Precisely when Henry Slaughter began his steamboat company is not clear, but it is believed to have been sometime around the mid-1850s. It appears that he eased into the business by teaming up with one or more of the independent steamboat operators of the day before attaining ownership. Slaughter's name first appears in an advertisement of February 28, 1857, as the proprietor of the steamer *Arrow*.[26] Under the command of Captain E.S.L. Young, she departed Baltimore every Saturday, Tuesday and Thursday morning at 8:00 a.m. with calls at the regular wharves. She left Crumpton every Monday, Wednesday and Friday morning at 7:00 a.m., departing Chestertown at 8:00 a.m., Rolph's Wharf at 8:30 a.m., Grey's Inn Creek at 10:30 a.m. and Queenstown at 11:30 a.m., with arrival in Baltimore between 3:30 and 4:00 p.m. Since the steamer did not then call at Centreville, Slaughter provided for a hack to take passengers from Centreville to Queenstown, where they could board. The cost of a one-way voyage was one dollar with meals extra. All freight had to be prepaid before being loaded aboard.

Since the start of steamboat service on the Chester River, steamers had been stopping at a wide variety of landings between Baltimore and Crumpton, some of which were towns, others of which were country wharves owned by local farmers. Not all wharves were visited on every voyage, and in later years especially, there were fixed itineraries where one steamer would call at one group of wharves while another stopped at others.

Crumpton, at the head of navigation on the river, is a small town originally called Callister's Ferry in the eighteenth century for the man who ran a ferry across the river at that point. The present name is believed to honor William Crump, owner of a large tract of land in the area. Packinghouses and canneries there relied on the steamboats to take their products to market in Baltimore. Heading downriver, the steamers called at Spry's, Deep Landing, Buckingham Wharf and Roundtop

Wharf. The latter was the seat of the Carmichael family and was, in the late nineteenth century, the location of one of the largest peach farms in the world.[27]

Then it was on to Chestertown, the Kent County seat, originally known as New Town and founded in 1706. Between Chestertown and Rolph's Wharf was Piney Grove in Kent County, where there was a farmhouse that had been built in 1773 that was one of several landings where steamers stopped only on signal, usually a flag hoisted on a pole at the end of a wharf. Rolph's Wharf, a few miles below Chestertown, was a country landing on the Queen Anne's County side named for the Rolph family, who held a number of important positions in the county. Rolph's Wharf today is a marina, beach and bed-and-breakfast in the venerable River Inn. Crossing to the Kent County side, a steamer would next visit Riverside Wharf, home today to the Kent School but during earlier times the site of the Colonel E.M. Wilkins farm. Booker's Wharf was located on the Queen Anne's side between Southeast Creek and the Corsica River and was the wharf belonging to Dr. T.N. Booker. Today, it is the site of Camp Pecometh, a Methodist Church camp.

Farther along the Kent County shoreline is Quaker Neck Landing near the village of Pomona. The name is believed to have come from a nearby Quaker meetinghouse that dated from the late seventeenth century. Indiantown is a locale in Queen Anne's County where a wharf was located between Spaniard Neck to the southwest and White Cove to the northeast. The name might have originated with the Ozinie Indians, a branch of the Matapeake tribe on Kent Island. Indian artifacts and burial sites have been identified in this area. Grey's Inn Creek on the Kent side of the river is between Eastern Neck Island to the west and the Kent mainland to the east. The landing there served a number of farms in that vicinity. There was also a wharf at Cliffs on a peninsula bounded by Langford Creek and the Chester River that the steamers visited occasionally. The name most likely came from the configuration of the land in the area. Today, it is called Cliffs City and is the site of a public boat launch. Spaniard Neck was an occasional call for steamers, almost directly across the Chester from Cliffs. It shows up only occasionally in the schedules of the various Chester River steamboat operators. On the Queen Anne's side prior to Spaniard Neck, Ashland Landing was another farm wharf where vessels stopped only on signal. After rounding Spaniard Neck, a steamer would bear to port and enter Corsica Creek (today called the Corsica River) headed for a landing. In earlier days, the landing in this area was simply referred to as Corsica. Centreville has been the Queen Anne's County seat since 1782, and its town wharf was home to not only steamboats but also sailing vessels, many of which were owned and operated by Captain John Ozman, a well-known local shipping man. Three distinctive homes, called Captain's Houses, that he built along the banks of the Corsica near Centreville Wharf still stand today. Bogles Wharf was the landing for Eastern Neck Island, the ancestral home of the Wickes family and a piece of land that was especially well suited to farming.

Some of these wharves were small businesses unto themselves, and in several cases, they were incorporated by the General Assembly, such as the Quaker Neck Wharf Company. Such entities primarily managed the comings and goings of freight.

Queenstown, founded in 1706 and the first county seat of Queen Anne's County, is located on the banks of Little Queenstown Creek, an arm of the Chester, and was a port of call for Chester River steamers from the earliest days. It had a very long pier that reached out into the creek beyond the shallows, and there was also a packinghouse, granary and freight shed along the town's waterfront. Until steamers began stopping at Centreville, many steamboat patrons from there had to travel overland to Queenstown to meet the boat.

As the steamer neared the mouth of the Chester River, two landings in Queen Anne's County remained. Jackson Landing was a few miles southwest of Queenstown on Jackson Creek near an outcropping of land known as Long Point. This location was just east of Kent Narrows and was the wharf used by many of the farms in the area of what is now known as Grasonville. Jackson Landing today is a small public park. Then it was back to the main stem of the Chester as the steamer made her way to the eastern side of Kent Island, where she tied up at a wharf about halfway between Stevensville and Love Point at the tip of the island. Many people have assumed that the only steamboat landing on Kent Island was the one at Love Point, but that was not the case. Today, the area is still marked as Chester River Landing on local maps, and there is a road next to the river named Old Steam Ship Road.

Following departure from Kent Island, steamers would sometimes head directly for Baltimore and at others would cross the mouth of the river to call on the Kent County bayfront town of Rock Hall. Founded in 1707, it was a major port for the shipment of tobacco in earlier times and seafood and farm products in later years. Rock Hall was the last landing on the Eastern Shore before the steamers headed across the Bay for Baltimore.

The average steamboat wharf along the Chester would have consisted of a plain wooden pier with perhaps one or two buildings—one for use by passengers waiting for the boat and the other for the storage of goods awaiting shipment. Some had granaries, warehouses or canneries located on them. Nearly all had a pen nearby where animals scheduled for shipping could be held. On some rivers in the Chesapeake region, steamboat wharves had to be built far out into the river where it was deep enough for a vessel to come alongside. Most of the Chester River landings, however, were fairly close to shore because there was sufficient water. Docks that extended far offshore, however, could be found at Bogles Wharf on Eastern Neck Island and in Queenstown.

Henry Slaughter's boat the *Arrow* was built in 1855 in New Castle, Delaware, and was 123 gross tons. Like the vessels that preceded her, she was a combination passenger and freight steamer and would be a staple of Slaughter's fleet for many years. Service to the Chester River from Baltimore was still not daily in the second part of the 1850s—daily service was still a few years in the future. The *Arrow*'s schedule called for her departure from her Light Street dock in Baltimore on Saturday, Tuesday and Thursday mornings. She would call at many of the landings and end her voyage in Crumpton. Departures from Crumpton were on Monday, Wednesday and Friday mornings. This schedule remained in effect for some years, and Slaughter's boat became one of the most reliable and popular on the river.

At some point in the late 1850s, Slaughter acquired the *George Law* to operate with the *Arrow*, and she would remain on the route until 1886. A vessel 147 feet long on a beam of 42 feet, the *George Law* had been built in 1852 and was 266 gross tons. She appears to have been a very sturdy and reliable vessel that could go in all kinds of weather. Since no pictures appear to have survived, it is believed that she may have been of similar design to the *Hugh Jenkins*. It may also

RESUMTION OF TRAVEL!
For Chester River.

THE STEAMER "ARROW,"

CAPT. E. S L. YOUNG, on and after Saturday the 28th of Feb'y. will leave her wharf, Light street, every SATURDAY, TUESDAY, and THURSDAY MORNING for CHESTER RIVER at 8 o'clock. Returning will leave CRUMPTON every MONDAY, WEDNESDAY and FRIDAY MORNING at 7, Chestertown at 8, Rolph's 8½, Grey's Inn Creek 10½, Queenstown 11½, and arrive in Baltimore at 3½ to 4 o'clock.

☞ Passage $1. Meals extra.
☞ All freights prepaid.
Capt. John North. Agent at Baltimore.
    H. B. SLAUGHTER, Propietor.
☞ A HACK from Centreville connects with the boat at Queenstown Passengers can be taken to any point on the Shore.
February 23. 1857—tes.

This appears to have been the first advertisement for Henry Slaughter's steamboat *Arrow*, the first vessel of the Slaughter Line. *From the* Kent News.

Henry Slaughter had a cannery and other businesses across the river from Crumpton. This one was across from Crumpton and might be his. *Courtesy of Kevin Hemstock.*

have been during this time that the Slaughter Line began operating steamers on a daily basis, except Sunday, with one leaving Baltimore in the morning at the same time the other was departing from Chestertown.

Slaughter's steamboat business flourished, and by 1860, he was thinking that it was time for a brand-new steamer. Up to that point, all the boats operating on the Chester had been secondhand. Slaughter and his business associates drew up plans for a side-wheel passenger and freight steamer with a wooden hull and superstructure. While most official sources state that she was built in Chestertown,[28] there are a few accounts that say she was built in Crumpton, near the owner's by then prosperous farm. She was named the *Chester*. Although the vessel's hull and superstructure were built on the banks of the Chester in 1860 and 1861, she was then towed to Baltimore, where her steam engine and other mechanical equipment were installed by noted engine builder Charles S. Reeder. The fact that she was not built at a shipyard in a major port suggests that Slaughter and his associates must have either had knowledge of marine design or brought in a marine architect. Virtually all other steamers on the Chesapeake Bay had been built in yards in Baltimore or Wilmington, Delaware.

The *Chester* was a very handsome steamer of four decks, three of which were above the waterline. The engine, boilers and other large mechanical equipment were on the deck below the waterline. The first deck above the waterline is referred to on Bay steamers as the freight deck, since this is where most of the freight was carried. The front portion of that deck, forward of the pilothouse, was open on the sides and is where large quantities of fruits and vegetables from Eastern Shore farms were carried. Sometimes, a canopy was rigged over this open section of deck. The middle section of the

The first steamer built exclusively for service on the Chester River was Henry Slaughter's handsome *Chester*, which came out in 1861. *The Mariners' Museum, Newport News, Virginia.*

freight deck was enclosed, and near the middle of it was the huge, brightly decorated paddle box that covered the boat's paddle wheels. Paddle boxes were real works of art in the nineteenth century, and little effort was spared to make them as colorful as possible. They usually had designs that radiated out to the edges of the semicircular paddle boxes from an intricate carving right above the vessel's name. The steamer's name was painted in bold letters just beneath the paddle box design, and it is interesting to note that there was a period at the end of the name. The area at the extreme stern with windows all the way around might have been the dining room, but unfortunately, no plans survive of the *Chester.*

The next deck up was called the saloon deck not because it was a place to obtain liquid refreshment but because it housed the central passenger space, usually an open area that in those days was called the saloon. The pilothouse was at the front of the third deck above the water—usually called the gallery deck—and for at least part of the boat's career, it was surmounted by a gold-painted carved eagle. Behind the pilothouse was the tall single funnel, and behind that was the walking beam, one end of which was attached to the paddle wheel shaft and the other end to the steam piston mechanism of the engine.

Upon completion, the *Chester* steamed back to Chestertown and met with a very positive reception upon arrival:

> She may be justly regarded a model boat, and her accommodations are ample…The public may now feel assured of a reliable daily conveyance between Chestertown and Baltimore. Capt. E.S.L. Young, formerly of the Arrow, *takes command of the* Chester, *and Mr. B.S. Ford, the efficient clerk of the* Arrow, *has been promoted to the captaincy of that boat.*[29]

The term "reliable daily conveyance" is apparently one of the first mentions in print of daily service by Slaughter's steamboats. In those days, the *Chester* operated between Baltimore and Chestertown and the *Arrow* between Baltimore and Crumpton. These two vessels were to constitute the fleet of the Slaughter Line for the next several years. Budd Sterling Ford, mentioned as the new captain of the *Arrow*, would eventually become a major player in the steamboat business on the Chester River and would even have a steamer named for him.

DAILY LINE
FOR CHESTER RIVER.

On and after Friday, April 12th, the Steamer ARROW, Capt. B. S. Ford, and the new Steamer CHESTER, Capt. E. S. L. Young, will leave alternately their wharf, Light street, daily at 8 o'clock, A. M., touching at the different landings. Returning, the Arrow leaves Crumpton at 7 o'clock, A.M., and the Chester leaves Chestertown at 8½ o'clock, A. M.

Fare $1—meals extra.

H. B. SLAUGHTER,

apr20.   Proprietor.

Daily service became a reality for the first time in 1861, when the *Chester* and *Arrow* began operating in tandem for Henry Slaughter. *From the* Kent News.

Even though the Slaughter Line was the main operator of steamers on the Chester River, there was still competition from occasional independent operators. A gentleman named Isaac Winchester advertised a two-boat service beginning a month after the *Chester* entered service. The record is unclear, but it appears that he may have bought the two boats at a court-ordered auction of the fleet of the Eastern Shore Steamboat Company, which was experiencing financial difficulties at that time. Bids had been received for the company's vessels in April 1861. Winchester's service was not daily and called for the *Hugh Jenkins* to leave Baltimore every Thursday for Chester River points and the steamer *Balloon* every Monday, Wednesday and Saturday, both returning to Baltimore the same day. When she wasn't running on the Chester, the *Balloon* was steaming to Annapolis and West River points on Tuesdays and Fridays. The *Balloon* was an older boat of 204 tons, having been built in 1854 in New York. She operated sporadically on the Chester River for several years and went on to serve the Federal government during the Civil War. Winchester's operation must not have been a success, however, because there is no mention of it after late July 1861.

There were occasional mishaps, but they appear to have been few over the years and not terribly serious. One occurred on March 24, 1863, as the *Arrow* headed for Crumpton. For some unknown reason, she clipped the drawbridge over the Chester River at Chestertown and damaged the port side wheel, forcing her to lie alongside the bridge for several hours while damage to both boat and bridge were assessed. Fortunately, no one was injured. She eventually made it to Crumpton with one side wheel and deft maneuvers of the rudder. The next day, she came back downriver and made it to Baltimore on just one wheel. The damage to the steamer was put at between $400 and $500. One can only wonder what such a repair would cost today.[30]

A vessel appeared as part of the Slaughter Line's fleet in April 1864 that is quite the mystery ship. She was named the *Minna* and was described as a "handsome boat with a large saloon on the upper deck."[31] She was paired with the *Chester* until April 1865, when she left the fleet. Although it was said that the *Minna* was to replace the *Arrow*, which briefly left the company, the *Arrow* returned to the Slaughter fleet in December 1864 and joined the *Chester* and the *Minna*. The only record that can be found in either *Merchant Vessels of the United States* or the *Lytle Holdcamper List* of a vessel named *Minna* is a British-built blockade runner captured near Charleston, South Carolina, in 1863, and she is listed as a sailing vessel. The *Minna* is mentioned in the

Kent News in April 1864 as a fine new steamer and in July 1864 as having been taken over by the Federal government. The full story of the *Minna* remains a mystery.

The Baltimore terminal of the Slaughter Line was on Light Street at the foot of Conway Street, right in the middle of the city's bustling steamboat waterfront. In those days, steamboat wharves stretched from the vicinity of Federal Hill—near where the Maryland Science Center is today—up Light Street and on to intersecting Pratt Street, where Harborplace is located today. Light Street was narrow with wharves on one side and warehouses, dry goods stores, fruit-packing buildings and offices on the other. The street itself was almost always cluttered with horses and wagons delivering freight and passengers to the many steamers tied up there. The Light Street piers were among the busiest in the port of Baltimore. Things got even busier in the late afternoon and early evening, when most of the overnight steamers departed, and again early in the morning, when others arrived and unloaded passengers and freight. Pier 7, Light Street, was home to the Slaughter Line with a large front area where wagons could be backed up and loaded and unloaded. Passengers had to make their entry into the pier through a small door on one side of the building.

As for the ports of call along the river, Queenstown's pier had a shed at the end. Nearby, there was a large granary and warehouse. The Centreville wharf was alongside a bulkhead, and there were a number of freight buildings nearby. Chestertown's wharf was at the foot of High Street, and it was known as the "Steamboat Wharf," located next to another one called the "County Wharf." Here again, there were several buildings on the pier for storage of freight and to provide shelter for passengers. At Crumpton, the wharf was on the Queen Anne's County side of the river next to a freight shed or two. There was also a cannery and other facilities on the Kent County side of the river, the goods from which were shipped on the steamers. The other wharves were primarily short, wooden piers extending out a short distance from the shore, with sheds at the end.[32]

The mid-1860s saw a fair amount of competition on the Chester River route. While the Slaughter Line was unquestionably the top line, competitors appeared several times during that decade. In October 1864, a concern calling itself the New Chester River Line appeared, operated by Captain J.F. Taylor and using a steamer named *Isadore*. She was a new boat of 127 gross tons, built that year in Baltimore. She advertised the carrying of freight at moderate rates and departed from Baltimore on Tuesday, Thursday and Saturday. With the introduction of the *Isadore*, it didn't take long for a rate war—a phenomenon that almost always followed a new boat—to develop. Practically the same week that the New Chester River Line began operations, the Slaughter Line countered with a small reduction in fares and beefed-up service. It placed three of its four steamers—the *Chester*, *Arrow* and *Minna*—into daily (except for Sunday) operations from Crumpton to Baltimore. The *George Law* was placed on a daily route between Centreville and Baltimore. The New Chester River Line continued to run in opposition to the Slaughter Line until March 1866, at which time the *Isadore* was taken off the run and relocated elsewhere.

With the end of the Civil War, the Slaughter Line, despite occasional competition, found itself in an enviable position with a well-rounded fleet and plenty of freight and passenger business. Although railroads were beginning to appear, the steamboat remained the preferred method of transportation.

However, tragedy intruded on this picture of prosperity.

Henry B. Slaughter died at his Crumpton home on October 26, 1865, the victim of typhoid fever. He was forty-eight years old and had been ill for ten days. His death stunned communities along the Chester River as well as his colleagues in the shipping business. Tributes referred to him as a much-respected and valuable citizen of Queen Anne's and Kent Counties:

> *The deceased was a man of the strictest integrity and honor, of warm and generous impulses, and always kind and benevolent. In his death the church has lost a most worthy and consistent member, the poor a true friend, his family a devoted husband and father, and our community one of its most useful and upright citizens.*[33]

He was further described as a man possessing a "bold and enterprising mind" and the head of a steamboat company that "has proved to be one of the most successful and popular lines ever established on our river."[34] The *Sun* in Baltimore also praised Slaughter, saying that he was "well known and respected in this city" and was "one of the most enterprising men of his time."[35]

Despite the death of its founder, the Slaughter Line continued to move forward. However, when a public sale of Henry Slaughter's estate took place on November 28, 1865, the steamboat line was not one of the assets placed up for sale with his animals, farm implements, furniture and the like by Joel C. Slaughter, Henry's son, executor of his estate and the man who took over management of the Slaughter Line with plans to continue operating the steamers.

In the years that he operated his steamboat company, Henry Slaughter never incorporated it, something that Joel C. Slaughter, B.S. Ford and others set out to do in 1867. That year, the Maryland General Assembly enacted legislation naming Slaughter of Kent County; Ford of Queen Anne's County; and John J. Shabb, Jacob Barkman and Samuel M. Lawder of Baltimore City commissioners "to receive subscriptions and payments for the shares of capital stock of the said corporation."[36]

They must have adequately fulfilled their charge from the General Assembly, for on February 18, 1867, an act incorporating Slaughter's Steamboat Company was passed. The enabling legislation also stipulated that the capital stock of the new corporation not exceed $150,000 and that shares be sold for $100 each.[37]

Here, however, the waters get muddied. In the same legislative session, the General Assembly also enacted a bill incorporating the Chester River Steamboat Company, a wholly new corporation. It was to be operated by Thomas D.C. Ruth and George B. Westcott of Kent County and William McKenney and John C. Ruth of Queen Anne's County. The Chester River Steamboat Company began operations on August 2, 1867, with the steamer *Kent Island*, the one-time *Hugh Jenkins* that had recently undergone a major overhaul, including installation of a modern boiler that its advocates assured patrons would not explode. Boiler explosions, which had been commonplace at the time when steamboats were first developed, still occurred on occasion. The Slaughter Line was then operating the *Chester* and the *George Law* between Baltimore and Crumpton.

The Chester River Steamboat Company must have kept the *Kent Island* for only a short time because she shows up in October 1867 as being independently operated by Captain J.A. Burgess on the same route. At some point, the *George Law* was disposed of by the Slaughter interests because she was advertised in May 1869 as a vessel of the Chester River Steamboat Company, of which the aforementioned Budd Sterling Ford had become president. Prior to taking up her duties for her new owners, she underwent considerable renovation, including the addition of a copper bottom, a new boiler, improved saloons and improved staterooms (actually day rooms, since the run was a daylight one). She was under the command of Captain Phineas Samuel McConnor.[38] Initially, she was the only steamer of the new line, but soon, the *Chester* joined her, as the Slaughter Line wound down its operations.

It quietly disappeared from the scene in May 1869.

4.

THE CHESTER RIVER STEAMBOAT COMPANY

Be it enacted by the General Assembly of Maryland, That Thomas D.C. Ruth and George B. Westcott of Kent, and William McKenney and John C. Ruth of Queen Anne's county, their associates, successors and assigns be and they are hereby created a corporation and body politic, by the name and style of the "Chester river Steamboat Company," and by that name may have perpetual succession… [39]

So read the opening section of *An Act Entitled, an Act to Incorporate the Chester River Steamboat Company* that was passed by the Maryland legislature on January 11, 1867. The bill set the capital stock of the new company at not more than $50,000 with shares at $100 each. The act of incorporation gave the owners and operators the authority to buy or build steamboats and to purchase or rent "and hold all necessary wharves, buildings, materials… which may be required for the [*sic*] conducting the business of a new Steam passenger and Freight Company." [40]

Since the existing Chester River steamers were in the possession of the Slaughter Line, which was in the process of being incorporated by Henry Slaughter's heirs, the newly formed Chester River Steamboat Company had to look elsewhere for vessels. It succeeded in obtaining the steamer *Kent Island*, which was no stranger to the Chester River, since she had operated there prior to the Civil War as the *Hugh Jenkins*. During the war, she became the property of the U.S. Quartermaster Department and served with Union forces through the remainder of the war. In 1866, she was renamed the *Kent Island*.

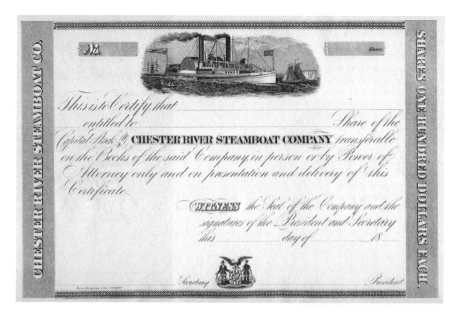

The Chester River Steamboat Company was incorporated in 1867, with stock shares going for $100 each. The image, however, is not a Chester River boat. *Author's collection.*

The *Kent Island* made her first trip between Chestertown and Baltimore on August 2, 1867, making all of the regular landings between those two places. The company's first advertisement called her a "fine, large steamer having been rebuilt and thoroughly repaired."[41] It went on to praise her new boiler, which the Franklin Institute in Philadelphia had examined and declared to be non-explosive. "Those, therefore, who patronize this boat may be well assured of their safety from any steam explosion," the advertisement stated.[42]

No doubt the competition was keen on the Chester River with the two companies offering virtually identical services. Fares on both lines were $1.25, and meals were extra. It is not difficult to imagine steamers of each line running close to the other on their way to either Baltimore or the Chester River with passengers on each calling across to the other and extolling the virtues of their boat.

This competition continued into 1869, by which time the fortunes of the Slaughter Line were apparently in decline, as the Chester River Steamboat Company became more firmly entrenched and emerged as the leading line on the river.

No advertisements appeared for the Slaughter Line after May 8, 1869, and the steamer *George Law* was listed a few days later as then being owned by the Chester River Steamboat Company. Her new owners gave her a thorough overhaul, including a copper bottom, a new boiler, improved staterooms (dayrooms) and a fresh coat of paint. She was under the command of Captain P.S. McConnor, veteran Chester River steamboat man.[43] News accounts at the same time reported that the *Chester* was also owned by the new company and was undergoing renovations similar to those undertaken on the *George Law*. The schedule for the coming summer season called for the steamers to depart at 7:00 a.m, one in each direction, making all landings below and including Chestertown and continuing on to Crumpton. Departure from Crumpton the next morning was at 6:30.

Heading the Chester River Steamboat Company was Budd Sterling Ford of Queen Anne's County, who would become known as one of the most respected steamboat owners in the Chesapeake region. Born in Salem, New Jersey, in 1840, he was forced to leave school at fourteen following the death of his father and worked for about a year as a clerk in a wholesale drugstore in Philadelphia. Following a brief period working in Ohio, he returned to Maryland and was hired as a clerk on steamers of the Slaughter Line. He quickly rose through the ranks and became a steamboat captain in 1860. Two years later, he married and left the steamboat company with the objective of becoming a farmer in Queen Anne's County, "but this, he found on trial was not suited to his disposition or his tastes."[44] When that didn't work out, he returned to the steamboat business and was one of those instrumental in securing the incorporation of the Slaughter Line. At some point, he made the transition to the new Chester River Steamboat Company and became its president.

In 1872, he was elected to the Maryland House of Delegates from Queen Anne's County and served a two-year term, and then in 1875, he was elected to a four-year term as state senator for Queen Anne's County. He was described as "a man of decided ability and influence, both in business and politics."[45]

Among the other incorporators, William McKenney of Centreville was a well-known financier in Queen Anne's County and president of the Centreville National Bank from 1876 to 1897. His other transportation interest was helping to build the Queen Anne's and Kent County Railroad. George B. Westcott of Chestertown was a bank bookkeeper and farmer for many years before succeeding his father in the mercantile business.

The Chester River Steamboat Company disposed of the *Kent Island* after obtaining the *Chester* and *George Law*. The *Kent Island* found employment elsewhere in the Chesapeake and was finally abandoned at an unknown

This was the Chester River Steamboat Company's first pier in Baltimore as it appeared around 1870. Are the wood piles coming or going? *Robert G. Merrick Collection of the Maryland State Archives.*

location in 1877. Although the company was by this time the undisputed leader on the Chester, competing operations still appeared occasionally. In July 1869, a concern called the Philadelphia and Chester River Steam Transportation Line appeared on the scene to carry peaches and other farm products to markets to the north. The company obtained the screw steamer *Com. H.A. Adams* to make triweekly trips between Chestertown and the City of Brotherly Love. She departed Chestertown in the evening and was in Philadelphia the next morning, transferring her peach cargo to the Camden and Amboy Railroad, which carried it on to New York.[46] There was another company billed simply as the Daily Peach Boat with evening departures from Chestertown for Baltimore with stops at Rolph's, Booker's and Quaker Neck Landings. The unidentified steamer was said to have a capacity of five thousand boxes of peaches. And even in this latter half of the nineteenth century, sailing vessels continued to offer freight service from river points to Baltimore.

In addition to its regular runs, the line occasionally offered other services, such as on July 7, 1870, when the *Chester* ran a special all-day excursion from Chestertown to Cambridge and back. It stopped at all the regular river landings to pick up passengers, who were treated to a catered dinner and refreshments. But there was no alcohol available. The company made it plain that the bar would be closed and no alcoholic beverages would be permitted on board. "No efforts will be spared to make this one of the most pleasant excursions that ever went from Chester River," advertising copy stated.[47] In September 1870, during the weeklong cattle show in Chestertown, it altered its schedules to accommodate those visiting the show and also charged a special round-trip fare of two dollars.

At this point in the company's history in the early 1870s, it listed a number of managers answering to B.S. Ford. They included George E. Harrison, Samuel Mallalieu, Jesse K. Hines, William A. Vickers, Lloyd Tilghman, Samuel J. Wickes and others representing many of the old families of Kent and Queen Anne's Counties.

It was during this period that the company improved its facilities in Baltimore. Its dock was located at Pier 7, Light Street—as had been the Slaughter Line's—almost directly across from where the Hyatt Hotel now stands. It leased the property from Abell and Walsh, who operated a large warehouse directly across Light Street that funneled freight to the steamers. The earlier pier of the Slaughter Line, as well as the Chester River Steamboat Company in its formative years, was a rather simple, one-story wooden structure through which passed both freight and passengers. In the early 1870s, the company tore that structure down and, within just three weeks, erected a new one that was a great improvement over the old. It was a two-story building with a fifty-seven-foot front on Light Street and sixty-two feet deep. It was described as "one of the finest and most substantial of its kind in the city," and the hope was expressed that other steamboat companies would follow suit.[48] At the same time, the Chester River Steamboat Company was termed "exceedingly fortunate and successful" under the leadership of Budd Sterling Ford.[49]

The decade of the 1870s proved to be a prosperous period for the company, even though competition still sometimes appeared. For instance, in February

The steamboat piers in Baltimore were along congested Light Street. The Chester River pier is the one with the tall flagpole to the left of the distant tower. *Author's collection.*

1871, the steamer *Osceola* began a run from Centreville to Baltimore, promoting reduced freight rates and accommodation for passengers. Little is known of the vessel as there were ten ships named *Osceola* listed in *Merchant Vessels of the United States* at that time. She must have been an independently operated vessel, but she made only a brief appearance on the Chester.

As for the Chester River Steamboat Company, its vessels were in good condition, as were its wharf facilities. It provided a safe and reliable service all year round. The only significant incident in that period was when the *George Law* sank with little warning near Booker's Wharf on October 8, 1875. The steamer was approaching the wharf when, according to news reports, the piston rod broke and impacted the wooden hull with enough force to knock a large hole in it:

> *The boat sunk* [sic] *in ten feet* [of] *water within a few minutes, but the bow rested on a knoll, where the depth of water was not so great. Some sheep and calves on board as freight thus escaped being drowned. The saloon, on the after part of the main deck, is three feet under water.*[50]

No one was injured, and all those on board were taken off without incident and landed at Booker's Wharf. With the *George Law* resting on the bottom of the Chester River, it was up to the *Chester* to maintain the service by herself.

The sunken steamer was raised on October 29 and taken to Baltimore for repairs. Given the long period during which she was sunk, there was concern that her machinery might have been badly damaged by being immersed in water, but that turned out not to be the case. The *George Law* returned to service sometime in November 1875. Although there were mishaps from time to time, most appeared not to be serious and did not result in any loss of life, something that could not be said of all steamship lines in the 1870s.

As the middle of the decade approached, company officials felt it was time to evaluate their fleet with an eye toward possible new construction. It was about that time that railroads were starting to emerge as competitors that were around to stay, and it became necessary for the Chester River Steamboat Company to meet the challenge head-on. New and larger steamboats were always a major drawing card. Clearly larger and newer tonnage was in order.

5.

TRIUMPH AND TRAGEDY

irectors of the Chester River Steamboat Company, meeting in early 1876, decided that they wanted the best steamers possible in service on the Chester River. From the outset, the plan was for two nearly identical side-wheelers to be built a few years apart. The second boat would include improvements gleaned from the operation of the first. It was decided to award the contract for the first steamer to the Harlan and Hollingsworth Corporation of Wilmington, Delaware, venerable builder of many fine steamboats.

The directors agreed that she should be named the *B.S. Ford* after the man who had done so much to make the Chester River Steamboat Company the successful firm that it had become. The new *B.S. Ford* was to be of 417 gross tons, 164 feet in length and 27 feet wide with an iron hull. No one in 1876, however, could have possibly foreseen that she would turn out to be one of the longest-lived steamboats in Chesapeake Bay history.

Once the contract was awarded, construction moved ahead quickly on the banks of Delaware's Christina River. She was launched on May 8, 1877, and the event was quite a gala affair, as a large contingent of company officials and others traveled to Wilmington to witness the event. Young girls were often called upon to name steamboats, and the *B.S. Ford* was no exception. The ceremony was carried out by "a little daughter of Capt. Benson, the master builder,"[51] who was otherwise unidentified in accounts of the launching. One can only imagine the pride Budd Sterling Ford felt seeing the Bay's newest steamboat take to the water for the first time with his name on her bow.

Completing the steamer's engine, superstructure and other equipment took about six weeks more, and then she was ready for her trial runs.

Ford and Captain P.S. McConnor, who was to be her first master, were aboard on June 23 for the vessel's first trip under steam, a fifteen-mile run up the Delaware River, during which she was reported to have made seventeen miles an hour, much to the satisfaction of her builders and new owners. It was reported afterward that "Mr. Ford, Captain McConnor, and the builders all express themselves highly elated with the action of the boat, and believe she will become one of the fastest on the Bay."[52] Following acceptance ceremonies, the *B.S. Ford* departed from Wilmington at 10:00 a.m. on June 28, bound for Baltimore by way of the outside route offshore and then up Chesapeake Bay. She passed Cape Henlopen, Delaware, that afternoon and then encountered rough seas off the Delaware and Maryland coasts, still making good time, and passed Cape Henry at the mouth of the Bay at 5:00 a.m. on June 29. Her officers stated that her encounter with rough seas showed her to be a good sea boat. She docked at Baltimore's Fells Point that evening, and the invited guests who made the trip all praised the boat's performance and her amenities. Until she began service the first week in July, she remained at Fells Point, where the public was allowed to tour her.

The *B.S. Ford* was hailed from all sides as an outstanding steamer. Painted white overall, she was a four-deck vessel, the lowest deck given over almost exclusively to machinery and cargo stowage. The second deck, known as the freight or main deck, was open forward of the wheelhouse to provide plenty of space for carrying the thousands of peaches, tomatoes and other products of Eastern Shore farms. The middle section of the main deck outside the area occupied by the paddle wheel machinery was used to transport other large shipments of freight and livestock bound for market in Baltimore. Just forward of the paddle wheel on the starboard (right) side was a barbershop, and just behind the same wheel was the purser's office. Behind the paddle wheel on the port (left) side was the captain's stateroom. (Presumably, the livestock was kept far forward of the captain's accommodations and the public rooms on that deck!) At the after end of the main deck was the "Smoking Room" with windows on three sides. A ladies' parlor was also provided in the same general area. Below those two rooms was the dining saloon, a well-lighted and well-ventilated somewhat triangular-shaped room. There were two long tables capable of serving one hundred passengers at one time and elegant furniture to match that in the rooms above. A large kitchen and pantry were just forward of the dining saloon. The food served

At 164 feet in length, the *B.S. Ford* was the largest steamer on the Chester River to that time. The open forward deck was for freight. *The Mariners' Museum, Newport News, Virginia.*

on Chesapeake Bay steamboats was always a major draw, and the steamboat companies went to great lengths to promote their meals. Two staterooms for ship's officers were forward of the pantry on the port side.

The forward part of the third deck, known as the gallery or upper deck, included the main saloon, with windows that wrapped around the front of the superstructure:

> *This apartment is 100 feet long, 30 feet wide, and furnished in very handsome style. The floor is covered with Brussels carpet, and the seats, of which there are a good number, placed, [sic] around the panel work, are made of walnut or other hard and costly wood. The saloon is painted in white and delicate shades of green, cream and gilt, and lighted by two rows of windows, the upper being of stained and the lower white glass, producing a very pleasing effect.[53]*

The platitudes continued, describing the ample open deck space outside the saloon, both forward and aft of the paddle boxes, where there was plenty of space for promenading or enjoying a picnic meal brought from home by some passengers. The paddle boxes, which enclosed the paddle wheels, deserve special mention, for they were the one part of the vessel's exterior not all white. As with most side-wheelers of the time, the paddle boxes were quite colorful. In the case of the *B.S. Ford*, there was a small carving of an eagle in the center just above the vessel's name. Fanning out from that spot to the edges of the paddle boxes was a painted multicolored sunburst-type design. While many side-wheelers looked alike from a distance, a close-up view made it evident that the designs of the carving and the fan design varied significantly from boat to boat.[54] For instance, in the case of the *Emma Giles*, which would visit the Chester in the future, the paddle box carving was of a beehive.

The wheelhouse, complete with a gilded eagle on its top; the funnel; and the lifeboats were all located on the fourth deck, sometimes known as the hurricane deck. There was also plenty of open deck space where passengers could enjoy the salt air and the breezes often present on the Chesapeake. The total cost of what was described as "a splendid boat" was $75,000, a fairly sizeable sum for 1877.[55]

Following her inspection period at Fells Point, the steamer moved on to Chestertown, where she was again opened to the local populace, which also waxed ecstatic about her. Then, on July 4, she set out on her first trip from Chestertown with four hundred passengers aboard. There was a lot of interest along the river, and many people turned out to see her in her element for the first time:

> *The wharves on the route were crowded on the Nation's holiday to greet this Queen of the Chester by an immense throng of people from all sections of the surrounding country; many to embark and admire her symmetrical beauty. This event was hailed as a new era of comfort to the traveling public and a marked advance in the business of the company.*[56]

The *B.S. Ford* settled into her new schedule, running in tandem with either the *Chester* or the *George Law*. She proved to be a very popular vessel and gave extraordinarily reliable service, never missing voyages because of any significant mechanical breakdowns or other difficulties. The board of directors kept close tabs on her operation, tweaking things here and there and making notes that would be consulted for the construction of the second vessel, still several years in the future.

Left: Captain Washington Woodall, with his four-legged friend, was captain on Chester River boats and the ferries between Baltimore and Love Point. *Courtesy Chesapeake Bay Maritime Museum, H. Graham Wood Collection.*

Below: The *B.S. Ford* at high speed on the open waters of Chesapeake Bay. She was one of the fastest steamboats on the Bay. *By permission of the Historical Society of Kent County.*

Less than a year after the *B.S. Ford* entered service, the decision was made to sell one of the older vessels, and the board adopted a resolution on April 25, 1878, to sell the *Chester* and retain the *George Law*. This is somewhat surprising, given that the *Law* was over twenty-five years old and the *Chester* was only seventeen. Perhaps it was simply a business decision—a newer boat would bring a higher price on the market. The *Chester* was bought by the Sassafras Steamboat Company and operated from Baltimore to Buck's Neck and Worton in Kent County. She continued operating out of Baltimore under her original name until 1894, when she was sold to the National Park/Philadelphia Line for service on the Delaware River. She was renamed *National Park* and remained in that service until 1906, when she was abandoned.

Despite the introduction of a modern new steamer by the Chester River Steamboat Company, its position on the river continued to be challenged from time to time. In most cases, an opposition line would show up with the sole objective of carrying peaches and other fruits and vegetables to Baltimore. For instance, in the summer of 1879, a company calling itself simply the Peach Line began operations with the steamer *Commerce* from Chestertown and promised guaranteed delivery to Hughes' Wharf in Baltimore and sales of the product on a daily basis. The occasional competition never seemed to faze the Chester River Steamboat Company and, in most cases, lasted only a season or two.

Things were looking quite rosy for Budd Sterling Ford, who was the president of a thriving steamboat company; one of the largest landowners in Queen Anne's County, with fourteen farms totaling 3,500 acres; and a first-term state senator from Queen Anne's County. It was written of him that "the course of Senator Ford has been marked with unvarying success."[57] He was also getting ready to be married for the second time. His first wife, Emily, had died in April 1868, leaving him with two young daughters, and now he was preparing to take a second wife. He and Alice Emory, who was from a long-established Queen Anne's County family, were to be married in 1879. But then, tragedy intervened.

On July 20, 1879, while visiting Ocean City with members of the Emory family, including his fiancée, Budd Sterling Ford died in an accident in the surf. He was attempting to help Mrs. E.B. Emory—his fiancée's sister-in-law—get to the beach when he went under, according to witnesses. Alice Emory was on the beach and watched the tragedy unfold as friends tried to revive Ford without success. It was believed that he suffered a heart attack. He was thirty-nine years old.[58]

Funeral services were held on July 24 in North East, in Cecil County, ancestral home of the Fords for many generations. A large delegation of political and business figures attended, including Mayor Ferdinand C. Latrobe of Baltimore, representatives of the Maryland General Assembly and officials of a number of Baltimore-based steamboat companies. In a July 26 editorial, the *Kent News* called the death "a painful shock to the community" and called Ford "highly esteemed and respected." It also described his "many acts of kindness and charity" to those with whom he dealt in his several capacities.[59]

Budd Sterling Ford was president of the Chester River Steamboat Company until his untimely death at the age of thirty-nine in 1879. *From the* Kent News.

Meeting in Baltimore on July 28, a stunned board of directors of the Chester River Steamboat Company stated that, with Ford's death, "the company is not only deprived of the services of a most valuable and active executive officer…the State of Maryland has lost one of its most honored and useful citizens."[60] The board also directed that company offices be draped in black for thirty days. Business had to go on, and at the same meeting, George Warfield of Baltimore was nominated to become the new president.

Born into an old Maryland family in 1834, Warfield was involved in a number of business interests over the years, having worked in the pharmaceuticals field, as a carpenter and later as a building contractor. Many years after taking over the presidency of the steamboat company, he was sheriff of Baltimore City from 1901 to 1903 and was also elected to the city council. He served on the board of directors of the Chester River Steamboat Company under Budd Sterling Ford for a number of years before being named to succeed him. "Mr. Warfield is a man of marked business ability, owing his success to no inherited fortune nor to any concurrence of advantageous circumstances, but to his own sturdy will, steady application, tireless industry, and sterling integrity."[61]

At the dawn of the 1880s, the *B.S. Ford* and *George Law* were the regular vessels, and they were joined in June 1882 by the newly constructed three-deck *Corsica*, built for the company at Harlan and Hollingsworth's Wilmington yard. Twenty feet shorter than the *B.S. Ford*, the new vessel was the company's first to be propeller (screw) driven. She was primarily a freight boat, meant to supplement the existing fleet. Her holds were designed for the transportation of the all-important peach crop, and she had a capacity for eight thousand boxes of peaches. She had sleeping accommodations for twenty-six people, a saloon eighteen by twenty feet and a compact dining room that was only nine by twelve feet. Her appearance was in marked contrast to the side-wheelers—considerably narrower with a tall, thin funnel situated aft. She was built at a cost of $40,000. The *Corsica* was often based in Chestertown, where she met the steamer from Baltimore and freight and passengers destined for Crumpton and other upriver wharves transferred to her for the remainder of the trip. Being a smaller vessel, she was better suited to the upper river, where shoaling was a constant problem.

A competing line featuring a familiar name arrived on the scene during the first half of the 1880s. The Enterprise Line, with Joel C. Slaughter listed as president, began operating the steamer *Enterprise* from Crumpton to Baltimore, touching at many of the regularly served wharves, as well as some others. It also operated the steam barge *A.J. Whitney* between Baltimore and Ben's Point near Church Hill. According to steamboat

The *Corsica* was the company's first propeller-driven steamer and was designed primarily to carry freight. She could carry a small number of passengers. *Courtesy Chesapeake Bay Maritime Museum, H. Graham Wood Collection.*

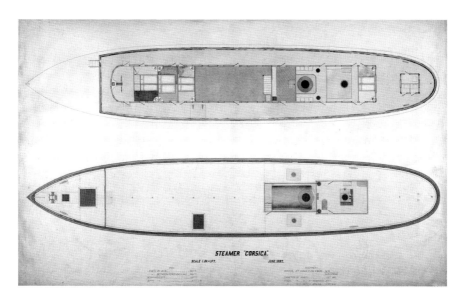

Deck plans of the *Corsica*. The passenger deck is shown in the top image and the freight deck is in the bottom image. *The Mariners' Museum, Newport News, Virginia.*

historians H. Graham Wood and Robert H. Burgess, the Enterprise Line represented "serious competition" for the Chester River Steamboat Company and flourished for several years.[62]

At about the same time, the company expanded its Chestertown wharf to include a 170-foot frontage on the river, and business was so good that it was decided to go ahead and plan the running mate to the *B.S. Ford* that had been anticipated for several years.

She was to be named the *Emma A. Ford* for Budd Sterling Ford's late wife. Although her given name was Emily, she apparently was known as Emma, the name with which the company chose to honor her. Once again, the contract was awarded to the Harlan and Hollingsworth Corporation. She was to be a near duplicate of the *B.S. Ford* in terms of layout but was longer at 180 feet on a beam of 30 feet. The company was anxiously looking forward to her debut because it would then own two of the most modern steamers on the Chesapeake.

But then disaster struck.

The *B.S. Ford* arrived in Chestertown on the afternoon of May 3, 1884, on her first trip following her annual overhaul. More than $2,500 had been spent on repairs and renovations that included a complete repainting and new upholstery. She was said to have never looked better and was ready

This excerpt from Fowler and Kelley's 1907 *Birds Eye View of Chestertown* shows the *Corsica* (bottom) and *B.S. Ford* approaching the High Street dock. *Author's collection.*

for a busy summer season. As was the usual routine, she was to spend the night at her wharf at the foot of High Street and depart for Baltimore the next morning.

At about 12:30 a.m. on May 5, fire broke out amidships and quickly spread throughout the vessel's wooden superstructure, no doubt fueled by the fresh paint and varnish. The officers and men who were spending the night aboard got ashore without injury, only to watch their beloved steamer be rapidly consumed by flames. Chestertown firefighters quickly arrived on the scene but could make little headway against the raging inferno. The steamer *Enterprise*, docked nearby, managed to get away from the dock and helped attempt controlling the fire with her fire hoses. Within two hours, however, the entire wooden superstructure was gone, and all that remained of the handsome steamer were her hull, engines and smokestack.

The company and the Chestertown community were thunderstruck by the loss of the steamer. The *Kent News* reported, "The *Ford* has always been a great favorite with our people—indeed, no boat has ever navigated the Chester which has been such a universal favorite with the traveling public."[63] Company president George Warfield, through an article in the local newspapers, thanked the town fire department and the citizens who helped battle the fire. As for the burned-out hulk, Warfield was not optimistic and said he did not think she could be salvaged or that her engines and other equipment could be used in a new boat.

In the aftermath of the fire, the *Corsica* joined the *George Law* on the regular run while company officials pondered their next move. It appeared initially that they were going to dispose of what was left of the *B.S. Ford* because at the June 1884 board meeting, the president of the company was authorized to sell her. One local news report referred to the *Emma A. Ford*, then under construction in Wilmington, as a replacement for the *B.S. Ford*, suggesting that the burned-out vessel would, indeed, be sold. However, after much soul searching, the decision was made to salvage what was left of the *B.S. Ford* and rebuild her, and she was taken to a Baltimore shipyard where the reconstruction took place. When she returned to service, she had the same general appearance as before, except that the forward end of the main deck, which had been open, was now enclosed.

Meanwhile, work went forward on the *Emma A. Ford*, and she was launched with appropriate fanfare on August 20, the naming honors going to Miss Helena A. Thomson. A large contingent of company and local officials attended, including Captain P.S. McConnor, who would take command of the *Emma A. Ford* as he had the *B.S. Ford* when she was new. She was completed about five weeks later and made her maiden voyage from Baltimore to Chestertown on October 7. She incorporated a number of interior changes that had been suggested by operating the *B.S. Ford*, and when she arrived at Chestertown for the first time, a crowd of between two and three hundred people cheered her.

The *Emma A. Ford*'s accommodations were described in glowing terms, especially the ladies' saloon, which "is tastefully carpeted, and the upholstery is crimson silk plush. The wood work in the ladies' saloon is in cherry."[64] All of the public rooms, it was noted by visitors, were larger than those on the

B.S. Ford. When asked about the vessel's performance, Captain McConnor replied, "Oh, she works like a charm. She handles beautifully."[65]

Having faced its share of highs and lows in less than a decade, the Chester River Steamboat Company had, by the mid-1800s, an excellent fleet of four steamers and was prepared for whatever the future might hold.

6.

A TRIP TO BALTIMORE ON THE *B.S. FORD*

There was hardly a ripple on the surface of the Chester River as the sun rose, turning the river into a sea of orange. Birds chirped as they flew overhead, and the workboats of river watermen were already out, having left their docks in the predawn hours. The town of Chestertown was still mostly quiet, but at the dock at the foot of High Street, things were anything but still. The gleaming white *B.S. Ford* was alongside the dock, her bow pointing downriver, wisps of steam drifting away from the tall black funnel as her engineers got steam up for departure to Baltimore. There were other boats along the Chestertown waterfront and out on the river, but the *Ford* towered over all of them.

Dockworkers were busy stowing freight in the holds and on the freight deck. It was summer, and the major freight at this time of year consisted of baskets and baskets of peaches and tomatoes from Eastern Shore farms. So many peaches were produced in Queen Anne's and Kent Counties in those days that the Chester River Steamboat Company often found it necessary to charter other steamers and barges to get the entire crop to market. Even as the loading went ahead, the clatter of wooden wheels on the wooden deck of the nearby Chester River Bridge echoed across the water as a last wagonload of produce made its way to the dock.

On the dock, a group of passengers waited for the signal to board. They were going to Baltimore for many different reasons. Some were businessmen going on behalf of their firms while others were planning to do some shopping at the many downtown department stores. The return trip might

The *B.S. Ford* at its dock in Chestertown. Its forward end was enclosed after it burned in 1884. The large house at right is Widehall. *Courtesy Chesapeake Bay Maritime Museum, H. Graham Wood Collection.*

see them with large bundles of clothes bought during their shopping sprees. Some were on the way to medical appointments and would come home with new supplies of medications. Others went to Baltimore to visit with relatives, and still others went for entertainment, attending performances at the city's many theaters.

Having been given the go-ahead to board, passengers streamed across the gangway onto the main deck and made their way to the purser's office, where tickets, costing fifty cents per person, were purchased. They were later collected as the steamer approached her Baltimore dock. Families often made their way to the open decks so they could watch as the dockworkers and deckhands hauled in the gangway, secured the loading ports in the vessel's side and prepared to let go the lines that held her to the dock.

Precisely at 7:00 a.m., the steam whistle let forth with a blast that echoed off the far shore and through the town, announcing that another trip to Baltimore was about to begin. There was a distant jangle of bells as the pilothouse signaled to the engine room that it was time to get underway. The lines were taken off the dockside cleats, and the huge paddle wheels began to slowly turn. Another blast on the whistle let other traffic on the water know that the big steamer was underway. The *B.S. Ford* moved quickly away from her dock, her paddle wheels rhythmically slapping the water as they propelled her forward. Children remained glued to the rails watching

The dock at the foot of High Street in Chestertown as seen from a departing steamer. *Courtesy Chesapeake Bay Maritime Museum, H. Graham Wood Collection.*

as the vessel picked up speed and the Chestertown waterfront receded in the distance. It was an event that happened every day, but for a young child making his or her first—or even second or third—trip to Baltimore, it was clearly something very special. And as the *B.S. Ford* headed downriver, the same drama was being repeated in Baltimore as the *Emma A. Ford* got underway for Chester River points.

Although the voyage from Chestertown had just begun, it was only a short time before the steamer rounded the first curve in the river with Piney Grove—an occasional stop—off to starboard and the section of the river known as Devil's Reach just ahead. It was a stretch that often gave sailing ship captains headaches due to a combination of shifting winds and shoals. But the *B.S. Ford* steamed through without difficulty and was soon in sight of Rolph's Wharf, the first of several country landings at which she would stop before reaching the mouth of the river, some twenty-five miles ahead.

Rolph's was typical of the wharves along the Chester River. In addition to the landing itself, it had a boardinghouse that remains today, two sheds, a blacksmith shop, a granary, a pasture and pens where animals waiting to be shipped were kept. Among those on the dock were farmers waiting to turn their fruits, vegetables and grains over to the shipping agent for transportation to market in Baltimore, where they hoped to get good prices. Passengers bound for the city came from the farms in the vicinity and were always

Rolph's Wharf was just a few miles below Chestertown on the Queen Anne's County side of the river. *Courtesy Chesapeake Bay Maritime Museum, H. Graham Wood Collection.*

dressed in their finest for their big trip. For many, it was as exciting as a deep-sea voyage. Depending on the amount of freight and the number of people boarding, the boat might stay at the wharf for as little as ten minutes or for more than a half hour before casting off.

The next regularly scheduled stop was at Quaker Neck Landing, a rural location that was an important transportation link for those living far outside any towns. Gilbert Byron, the renowned poet and author who grew up in Chestertown, was aboard once during the landing at Quaker Neck:

> *The first man to go ashore was a tall thin man who carried a little black box. He was the purser and it was his job to sell tickets to anybody who wanted to go to Baltimore. The deckhands began to bring the freight aboard, mostly fish, packed in ice, on two-wheeled trucks. They strutted and sang as they worked, just like they enjoyed it.*[66]

Quaker Neck and Rolph's were stops on every trip, but there were also a number of other landings where the steamers would only call if a signal had been run up on a pole at the edge of the dock. The signal could have been a white flag or a large ball. Such landings were Piney Grove, Indiantown, Ashland, Riverside, Spaniard's Point, Cliffs, Beck's, Earles, Puseys, Emory's, Wilmer's, Buckingham, Round Top, Deep Landing, Spry's and Grey's Inn

Left: A rare artifact of the Chester River steamers. This metal stencil was used to mark shipping crates being loaded at Rolph's Wharf. *Courtesy of H.F. "Chip" Winters Jr.*

Below: Rolph's Wharf had multiple buildings, including a blacksmith's shop, cannery, granary and boardinghouse. *By permission of the Historical Society of Kent County.*

Creek. A boat would stop at those locations only when a passenger wanted to get off or on or when a farmer had a shipment for the city.

Given the early hour of departure, many passengers went down to the dining room soon after leaving the dock to have breakfast. Meals on Chesapeake Bay steamboats were famous, whether they were breakfast, lunch or dinner. A typical breakfast would have offered such dishes as eggs, corn cakes with maple syrup, bacon, ham, rolls, fruits and coffee. If it was a special occasion, such as a holiday, the menu might also include potatoes, fish and an assortment of breads, juices and jams. The tables were set with

A deckhand prepares to toss a mooring line to workers on the dock. Note the anchor lying on the deck at right. *Photograph by the late W.C. Steuart, author's collection.*

Passengers gather at a steamer's rail to watch the docking and the loading and unloading of freight. *Photograph by the late W.C. Steuart, author's collection.*

fine linen, silver flatware and heavy china, and the passengers were waited on by highly efficient white-coated stewards.

As breakfast was served, the steamer continued downriver, passing rolling farmland, occasional farmhouses and one or two manor houses. Little wooden piers extended from the shore, and there were often pound nets reaching out into the river, to be worked by local watermen. The scene in the twenty-first century remains much the same. On nice days, many passengers spent most of their time on the open decks watching the passing countryside and observing the many watermen at work on the river. The large saloon offered comfortable chairs and settees from which to also view the passing scenery. During cold weather, it and the other public rooms were cozy places to observe the outside world in warmth.

Booker's Wharf was next and then Bogles Wharf on Eastern Neck Island (primarily a landing for freight), and sometimes after there, it was up the Corsica River to Centreville. More often than not, however, Centreville was served by another of the company's steamers based there. The next stop was Queenstown with its compact harbor where there was a long steamboat pier,

The Queenstown steamboat wharf was one of the longest along the Chester River because the harbor is so shallow. *Author's collection.*

Either the *B.S. Ford* or the *Emma A. Ford* is at the wharf at Quaker Neck Landing in Kent County. *Courtesy Chesapeake Bay Maritime Museum, H. Graham Wood Collection.*

a granary and other commercial buildings along the waterfront. The arrival of the steamboat there was an important event that always brought people down to the wharf.

Livestock bound for market was often loaded at Queenstown, and it was quite a sight for the passengers as they looked down from the upper decks watching deckhands pull, push and otherwise coax cattle onto the freight deck. Sometimes, in the case of reluctant sheep, the animals were picked up bodily by the deckhands and taken aboard. The sounds of sheep and cows occasionally emanating from the freight deck were part of the rest of the voyage.

A few miles farther on was Jackson Creek Landing, just east of Kent Narrows. It may be difficult to imagine today, but that part of Queen Anne's County was once sparsely populated. The arrival of the steamboat was a welcome event. Freight and passengers from what is now the Grasonville area would have boarded at Jackson Creek. After passing Kent Narrows, the steamer paralleled the western shore of Kent Island until it reached the island's landing, about halfway between Stevensville and Love Point.

Then it was across the wide mouth of the Chester to Rock Hall, the last stop on the Eastern Shore, where barrels of freshly caught oysters, fish

The luggage on the dock at Booker's Wharf suggests that this group is going to Baltimore for more than just a day trip. *Courtesy of Michael S. Kader.*

The arrival of a steamboat was always a major event. At Queenstown, passengers and freight wait for the steamer to tie up. *Courtesy of Michael S. Kader.*

Deckhands and dockworkers at Queenstown herd cattle onto a steamer's freight deck. *Courtesy Chesapeake Bay Maritime Museum, H. Graham Wood Collection.*

A ship's officer, at right, watches as dockworkers persuade a reluctant calf to get on the steamer. *Courtesy Chesapeake Bay Maritime Museum, H. Graham Wood Collection.*

or crabs, depending on the season, were loaded aboard for shipment to faraway destinations on the Western Shore by train or to Baltimore's finest restaurants. The wharf at Rock Hall was much larger than those on the river, and there was always a lot of activity there. The trip from Chestertown up to this point had taken about four hours:

> *And by that time, you were hungry. So you went into the spotless, shiny dining* [room] *where for 50 cents you got a meal of soft-shell crabs, fried chicken, all sorts of vegetables, salad, hot bread and coffee. By the time you'd finished, you were almost at Bodkin Point* [near the entrance to Baltimore Harbor].[67]

One former Chester River Steamboat Company officer recalled that mealtime, regardless of the time of day, was an event to remember. "Evenings it was like a social party in the cabin, with the captain doing the honors," he said.[68]

A steamboat in those days could not help but fire the imagination of young boys, some of whom envisioned themselves being steamer captains, resplendent in blue uniforms with gold braids. On more than one occasion, captains helped to cultivate that dream by taking youngsters under their wings during a trip down the river and across the Bay. On these occasions,

The *Emma A. Ford*, in Queenstown Harbor, was slightly longer than the earlier *B.S. Ford*. *Image ZN14.545.PP20, courtesy of the Maryland Historical Society.*

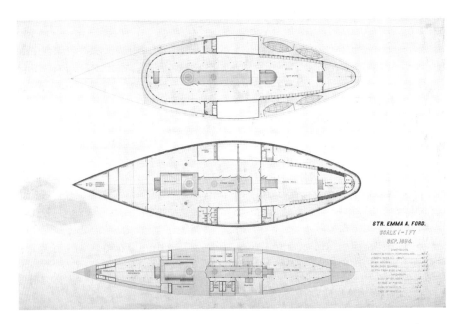

Builder's deck plans show the interior layout of the *Emma A. Ford*. The *B.S. Ford*'s interiors were similar. *The Mariners' Museum, Newport News, Virginia.*

the lucky boy would be brought up to the wheelhouse, that holy of holies where the captain reigned supreme, to watch and listen to the goings-on. Usually, the captain stood at a window to one side of the middle one, from where he had an unobstructed view of the waters ahead. A mate was often off to one side of the wheelhouse also keeping a lookout, and the helmsman deftly handled the huge wooden steering wheel from a spot in the center. There were several pieces of shiny brass equipment, including the engine room telegraph used by the captain to send orders and a binnacle that contained the steamer's compass. There were also brass spittoons.

The captain would explain the workings of everything in the wheelhouse, and as the young visitor watched, the captain would occasionally give an order for a change of course while the mate scanned ahead for the channel markers to help guide the steamer toward the mouth of the Patapsco River and Baltimore Harbor. The order was repeated by the helmsman once he carried it out, and then things became quiet again. Sometimes the captain would ask the boy if he wanted to take the wheel. The crowning glory of this visit came when the captain let him blow the whistle to signal another vessel. However, by the time the vessel approached the entrance to Baltimore Harbor, the boy would have departed, and it was all business again as the steamer entered the busy harbor with all its big seagoing ships.

Baltimore was one of the nation's busiest ports, and there were many steamships and sailing ships carrying a wide variety of cargoes to overseas destinations. Some of the ships were anchored while others were tied up at docks. There was activity everywhere for the passengers to watch as their boat steamed past Sparrows Point and into the Patapsco River. Tugboats of all shapes and sizes scurried around the harbor, their high-pitched whistles sounding. As the *B.S. Ford* steamed up the river, she passed a number of other steamboats headed out on their runs to ports on the Choptank, Nanticoke, Rappahannock, Potomac and York Rivers. Passengers, by now out on deck, waved and called to those on the passing steamers. Sometimes the captains saluted one another with a whistle blast or two.

Ahead lay the green expanse of Fort McHenry, which turned back a British invasion in 1814 and inspired Francis Scott Key to write "The Star-Spangled Banner." Up into the northeast branch of the Patapsco moved the *B.S. Ford*, slowing as she approached her Light Street dock. The captain deftly nosed her into Pier 7, and within moments, she was secured to the dock and the paddle wheels ceased their revolutions. Nearly seven hours had elapsed since the steamer had left Chestertown.

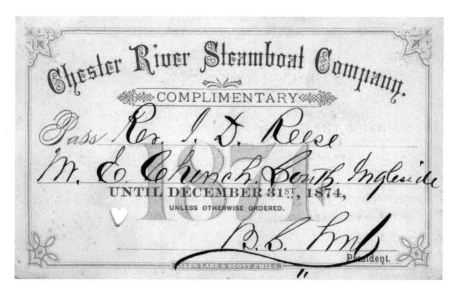

Steamboat companies issued passes to people with whom they did business. This one is signed by B.S. Ford. *Courtesy of the Mark Newsome collection.*

After the purser collected their tickets, the passengers went ashore to emerge into the hustle and bustle of a major city, a world apart from the rural life they had left behind on the Eastern Shore. Even before the passengers departed, the process of unloading the *B.S. Ford* had begun. Within a short time, the freight deck would be empty, awaiting the next shipments to come aboard in only a few hours, and the cycle would begin all over.

7

STEAMBOATS AND TRAINS TO THE OCEAN RESORTS

Decades before the Chesapeake Bay Bridge was built there was a transportation system in place that got Baltimoreans and Washingtonians to the ocean beach resorts through a pleasant combination of steamboats and trains, and did it in a pretty timely fashion. Just like today, people from the big cities of the Western Shore liked to visit the ocean resorts, but getting there was difficult and time consuming since most of the trip would have to be done overland on dusty or muddy roads. It was, of course, possible to take an overnight steamer from Baltimore to any point on the Eastern Shore, but then the traveler was pretty well on his own in arranging land transportation to the Delaware resorts, a bit of business that was quite time consuming.

There was also another part to the equation. Because the Pennsylvania Railroad was expanding its lines on the Delmarva Peninsula, many farmers on the Eastern Shore and in Delaware, as well as other businessmen, chose to ship their goods via that railroad through Philadelphia. Baltimore business interests felt they were losing out on a significant amount of business and wanted their share of it. The result was the formation of a combination steamboat-train route between Baltimore and the Delaware resorts and beyond.

The company known as the Queen Anne's Ferry and Equipment Company was organized in 1894 by businessmen from Maryland and Delaware to carry passengers by steamer from Baltimore's Light Street docks to Queenstown on the Chester River, where they transferred to a train to take them the rest of the way to Lewes and Rehoboth Beach. The trains were to be operated by the Queen Anne's Railroad Company.

It didn't take the Maryland General Assembly long to approve the project in the same year that the company was organized, but it took the Delaware legislature until 1897 to do likewise because the concept was being opposed by the Pennsylvania Railroad, which already had its own lines up and down the Delmarva Peninsula. Later on, the Pennsylvania Railroad would be a major player in the story of the steamboat on the Chesapeake Bay.

Besides being the transfer point from steamer to train, Queenstown was a destination unto itself. It was a quiet town of four hundred that traced its lineage to 1706, when it was the county seat of Queen Anne's County. At the time the Queen Anne's Ferry and Equipment Company and Queen Anne's Railroad began operations, the town had two hotels, a dance pavilion, a merry-go-round, swings for the children, a sandy beach and bathhouse and boats that could be hired for fishing and crabbing. The meals offered at the Hotel Bowlingly featured the best in Eastern Shore cuisine, including soft crabs, fried chicken, locally grown vegetables, hot bread, salad and coffee.[69]

It was a very efficient operation that had a steamer leaving Baltimore each day, once in the morning and then again in the late afternoon. The schedule called for the morning boat to depart from Pier 9½ on Light Street at 6:25 a.m. and arrive in Queenstown two and a half hours later. While crossing the Bay, passengers were treated to a hearty breakfast for only fifty cents. The transfer of passengers and their baggage to the train was handled expeditiously, and the train pulled out of Queenstown at 9:07 a.m. to make stops at twenty-two stations before arriving at Rehoboth Beach at 11:30 a.m. While the train was whisking its passengers to the beach, the steamer returned to Baltimore, often carrying freight that had earlier been brought to the Queenstown pier by the incoming train.[70] The steamer departed from Baltimore again at 3:40 p.m. to make the train connection at Queenstown, and it did it seven days a week at a time when many steamboats didn't operate on Sundays. However, there was only one departure in each direction on Sundays.

When one factors in today's traffic congestion around the big cities, traffic tie-ups at the Bay Bridge and other traffic issues, the steamboat-train schedule still looks pretty attractive—and a lot more pleasant.

The Queen Anne's Ferry and Equipment Company owned the steamers while the Queen Anne's Railroad Company owned the trains and the track. As part of their operating agreement, the steamboat line built terminals in Baltimore, Queenstown, Lewes and Rehoboth and leased them to the railroad.

The Queen Anne's Ferry and Equipment Company had planned from the outset to build a new steamer for the route and contracted with the Baltimore Dry Dock Company for a big side-wheeler to be named the *Queen Anne*. Her engine was built by Charles Reeder & Son of Baltimore, long known for superb steamboat engines. She was to be 210 feet long, with a beam of 30 feet on the hull and 50 feet over the guards. Her contract speed was to be about fifteen miles an hour, and her passenger capacity was 1,300. Staterooms were located on the saloon deck, second deck above the waterline. The cost of the new boat was $75,000.[71]

Work proceeded quickly on the *Queen Anne*, and she was launched on June 29, 1899, but the ceremony attending the naming of the boat was rather unusual. Normally, a new vessel was christened with champagne, wine or, in some cases, spring water but not the *Queen Anne*. She would enter the water without anything being broken over her bow. Instead, the young sponsor, identified only as Miss Gittings, named the vessel using the Japanese custom of releasing a flight of doves covered with white flowers at the moment of launch: "The doves, frightened by the blare of steam whistles, will circle away over the surrounding masts and the flowers will fall in a shower of fragrance and beauty on the deck of the new vessel."[72]

Although news accounts of the event went to great lengths to describe the tradition behind the releasing of doves at a ship's launching, it was never explained why that particular method was chosen for the *Queen Anne*. She was described as having "first class appointments throughout, including incandescent lights," a relatively new feature on Bay steamers.[73] She went into service near the end of the 1899 excursion season.

While the fitting out of the *Queen Anne* continued in Baltimore, forces were at work elsewhere that would eventually have a profound effect on the operations of the Queen Anne's Ferry and Equipment Company and the Queen Anne's Railroad Company. In September 1899, the Pennsylvania Railroad completed the purchase of the Baltimore, Chesapeake and Atlantic Railway, which ran a number of steamboat lines, including a steamboat-train combination between Baltimore and Ocean City, Maryland, with the transfer from boat to train taking place at Claiborne in Talbot County. That purchase meant that the Pennsylvania controlled all the rail lines on the Eastern Shore with one exception—the Queen Anne's Railroad Company. It would only be a matter of time before it, too, was absorbed into the sprawling Pennsylvania system.

The *Queen Anne* was completed at the end of October 1899 and, under the command of Captain William Storey, embarked on her trial run on October

The *Queen Anne* was built in 1899 to run between Baltimore and Queenstown for the Queen Anne's Ferry and Equipment Company. *Author's collection.*

26, 1899. The invited guests who made the trip were unanimous in their praise of the new boat. "Electric lights, searchlight and every feature of a modern steamer make the vessel the most complete of any of her class in the ports of the Atlantic," said the *Sun* in Baltimore.[74]

The *Queen Anne* entered service at the end of October 1899 and proved to be a very popular steamer, as new ones often were. She often engaged in unofficial races across the Bay between Baltimore and the mouth of the Chester River with the *Emma A. Ford.* Steamboat racing was not unique to the Baltimore–Queenstown route—it happened wherever there were competing companies. The captains never admitted to racing, and management often looked the other way; however, most passengers knew what was going on and lined the rails shouting at those on the other steamer. Initially, it was the *Queen Anne* that won the races, but later on, it was often the *Emma A. Ford* that reached the end of the run first.[75]

The *Queen Anne* was in service only a short time before the ice season set in, and it had always been intended that she would only operate in warmer weather. The company wanted to take no chances damaging its new boat in heavy ice, so it bought the twin-screw steamer *Endeavor* in

QUEEN ANNE'S RAILROAD COMPANY.
TIME TABLE.—In Effect Tuesday, October 28th, 1902.

EASTWARD.—Read Downward.						WESTWARD.—Read Upward.			
Saturday Only.	Daily Ex. Sat. & Sun.	Daily Ex. Sunday	Daily Ex. Sunday	Distance from Balto.	NAME OF STATION.	Daily Ex. Sunday	Daily Ex. Sunday	Daily Ex. Sat. & Sun.	Saturday Only.
P.M.	P.M.	A.M.	A.M.	Miles		A.M.	A.M.	P.M.	P.M.
2.00	3.15	....	6.15	....	Lv...Baltimore...Ar	11.40	....	9.00	7.40
3.55	5.10	....	8.10	25.00	Ar/Lv Kent Island Lv/Ar	9.40	....	7.00	5.40
4.00	5.15	10.45	8.20	28.81	....Stevensville....	9.32	10.23	5.58	5.05
4.07	5.22	11.00	8.29	30.44	....Chester....	9.24	10.13	5.48	4.56
4.10	5.25	11.15	8.32	....	....Narrows....	9.21	10.08	5.43	4.52
f 4.13	f 5.28	f11.18	f 8.35	34.70	....Winchester....	f 9.18	f10.03	5.38	f 4.48
4.18	5.33	11.30	8.40	35.82	....Walsey....	9.13	9.58	5.33	4.43
f 4.20	f 5.35	f11.33	f 8.43	38.07	....Queenstown....	f 9.10	f 9.54	5.24	4.39
4.25	5.40	11.40	8.49	38.07	....Queenstown....	9.04	9.48	5.18	4.33
4.45 / 4.00	5.58 / 4.50	11.57	9.20 / 8.35	44.26	Ar/Lv ..Centreville.. Ar/Lv	9.20 / 8.35	9.30	4.50	4.00
f 4.30	f 5.45	....	f 9.06	40.40	....Bloomingdale....	f 8.59	....	f 5.08	f 4.18
f 4.35	f 5.50	....	f 9.14	43.45	....Wye Mills....	f 8.53	....	f 5.01	f 4.11
f 4.42	f 5.56	....	f 9.22	46.43	....Willoughby....	f 8.47	....	f 4.52	f 4.02
....	6.04	....	....	....	..D. & C. Junction..	f 8.40	....	....	....
4.53	6.06	....	9.34	50.48	....Queen Anne....	8.38	....	4.30	3.49
5.00	6.12	....	9.42	53.68	....Downes....	8.32	....	4.30	3.40
f 5.04	f 6.15	....	f 9.46	55.05	....Tuckahoe....	f 8.29	....	f 4.29	f 3.37
5.11	6.21	....	9.55	57.99	....Denton....	8.24	....	4.20	3.30
5.17	6.27	....	10.10	60.89	....Hobbs....	8.18	....	4.04	3.14
5.26	6.35	....	10.20	64.57	....Hickman....	8.10	....	3.52	3.02
f 5.30	f 6.39	....	f10.24	66.40	....Adamsville....	f 8.06	....	f 3.44	f 2.54
f 5.35	f 6.44	....	f10.30	69.55	....Blanchard....	f 8.01	....	f 3.37	f 2.47
5.43	6.50	....	10.40	71.80	....Greenwood....	7.55	....	3.30	2.40
f 5.51	f 6.57	....	f10.55	75.47	....Owens....	f 7.47	....	f 3.00	f 2.10
f 5.56	f 7.01	....	f11.00	77.57	....Oakley....	f 7.43	....	f 2.55	f 2.45
....	....	....	11.05 / 11.15	81.07	Ar/Lv ..Ellendale.. Ar/Lv	7.86	....	2.48	1.53
6.04	7.08	....	f11.23	84.91	....Wolfe....	f 7.29	....	f 2.99	f 1.39
6.12	7.15	....	11.30	87.57	....Milton....	7.22	....	2.21	1.31
6.20	7.22	....	f11.40	91.57	....Whitesboro....	f 7.14	....	f 2.11	f 1.21
f 6.28	f 7.30	....	f11.43	92.82	....Overbrook....	f 7.11	....	f 2.63	f 1.18
6.31	f 7.33	....	11.52	96.82	Ar....Lewes....Lv	7.03	....	2.00	1.10
6.40	7.42	A.M.	P.M.			A.M.	A.M.	P.M.	P.M.

f Stops on signal to take on or let off passengers.

I. W. TROXEL, General Manager.   W. D. UHLER, Gen. Pass. Agent.

A 1902 timetable for the steamer/railroad operations of the Queen Anne's Ferry and Equipment Company and Queen Anne's Railroad. *Author's collection.*

A train that connected with the steamers at Love Point and Queenstown crosses Kent Narrows. *Courtesy Chesapeake Bay Maritime Museum, H. Graham Wood Collection.*

mid-December 1899. Built in 1896 in Philadelphia, she was described as a strongly constructed steamer that handled well in ice and could break through it with some ease. She could carry seven hundred passengers and 150 tons of freight. Once the *Endeavor* arrived in Baltimore from Philadelphia, certain improvements were made to the saloon and smoking rooms that were designed to bring her accommodations more in line with those on the *Queen Anne*, even though the *Endeavor* was significantly smaller. Once warm weather returned and the *Queen Anne* was back on the line, the company operated both steamers, with the *Endeavor* sometimes handling only freight. Having two vessels came at an opportune time because business was proving to be quite good and the companies had to turn away customers when it had only the one vessel.

In the midst of this period of prosperity, there were murmurs along the various waterfronts about the possible consolidation of the many individual steamboat lines then operating on the Bay. Speculation was that the Pennsylvania Railroad was behind such a move to acquire various steamboat lines and rail lines that competed with its Delmarva Peninsula operations. "Rumors galore" was the way the *Centreville Observer* put it.[76] It reported that one possible scenario had the Pennsylvania acquiring the Chester River Steamboat Company and extending the rails of one of its Delmarva subsidiaries to Rock Hall. By so doing, it could run a steamer from Baltimore to the railhead at Rock Hall in one and a quarter hours, compared to the *Queen Anne*'s time of two and a quarter hours from Baltimore to its rail connection at Queenstown. Officials of both the Chester River Steamboat Company and the Tolchester Steamboat Company, which operated from Baltimore to Tolchester beach north of Rock Hall, said they had not been approached about selling their companies. Nevertheless, the rumors persisted.

There was a report in March 1900 that the Queen Anne's Railroad was considering extending its line from Queenstown to Love Point on the northern tip of Kent Island in order to shorten the time of the steamboat crossing from Baltimore to about one hour. Love Point and Queenstown are about twelve miles apart.[77] It was also reported that there was the possibility of a boat crossing from Annapolis to Kent Island—the narrowest part of the Bay at four miles—to attract business directly from Washington through the state capital. Because Queenstown Harbor was shallow and its channel very narrow, docking steamers there took some time, and that delay would be eliminated by landing at Love Point instead. In fact, Queenstown Harbor was scheduled to be dredged the very next month. Queen Anne's Railroad president William H. Bosley denied that

The *Endeavor* was chartered and then bought by the Queen Anne's Ferry and Equipment Company pending completion of its new steamer. *Courtesy of the Ewen collection.*

the company was actively considering such a move but didn't say whether it might be considered at a later date.

With the rail line extended to both Lewes and Rehoboth, interests in Cape May, New Jersey, thirteen miles across Delaware Bay from Lewes, made plans to build a pier at Cape May so that a steamer meeting the train in Lewes could bring passengers to the New Jersey resort.

In August 1900, the Queen Anne's Railroad announced that it would, after all, extend its rail line to Love Point from Queenstown in order to provide faster service to the ocean resorts. It envisioned the one-way trip to take less than four hours. In addition to benefiting the passenger trade, the extension would improve the freight trade, with trains and boats carrying farm produce and other freight from the Eastern Shore to Baltimore.[78]

It was also noted that ice would be less of a problem at Love Point, compared with that in the small harbor at Queenstown, which, because it is surrounded on three sides by land, tended to freeze solid for long periods. Another factor was that production was up on farms on Kent Island and a pier closer to them would be beneficial in the shipping of farm products to Baltimore.

With the pending change of terminals, the Queen Anne's Ferry and Equipment Company decided that the time had come to build another new vessel to handle the Lewes–Cape May portion of the route.[79] The addition of a third steamer also gave it the flexibility to move vessels from route to route as traffic demanded.

The Baltimore Dry Dock Company was again chosen as the builder of a new single-screw steamer to be named the *Queen Caroline*. The contract stipulated that the ship be completed in time to begin her summer season the first week in July. The builders went to work, and the *Queen Caroline* was ready for launching on May 13, 1902. This time, however, the launch would be traditional and would not include doves. She was christened and named by Marie Bosley, daughter of William H. Bosley.

The new steamer was two hundred feet long with a beam of thirty-one feet and a draft of just under eight feet. Her triple-expansion engine was designed to drive her through the water at a speed of sixteen miles an hour, but she actually did much better than that once she settled in on her new route. Like the *Queen Anne*, she had six staterooms and was outfitted with white and gold decorations in the main saloon and a stained-glass dome overhead. There were oak staircases and a brightly lighted dining room on the main deck aft. "The *Queen Caroline* is a fine specimen of a modern-day

The *Queen Caroline* was the second vessel built for the Queen Anne's Ferry and Equipment Company. Here it is later in its career as the *Montauk*. *Courtesy of the Ewen collection.*

passenger steamer of the average size, which is most popular on short routes in American waters," stated the *Sun*.[80] The ship was delivered to her owners the first week in July 1902, as stipulated in the contract.

A few weeks before the *Queen Caroline* was delivered, the Queen Anne's Ferry and Equipment Company leased its three steamers to the Queen Anne's Railroad Company, furthering the close working relationship between the two firms. Under the new arrangement, the railroad was to pay the steamboat company $22,050 a year in monthly installments. There apparently were plans to eventually combine the two corporate entities into a single company.

With two modern steamers in regular service and a third one available to assist during heavy travel periods, the Queen Anne's Ferry and Equipment Company and the Queen Anne's Railroad settled into what was expected to be a long-term period of prosperity. But at some point, financial difficulties set in, and in February 1904, a receiver was appointed for the railroad. It was said to be an "amicable" proceeding with the goal of reorganizing the railroad and steamboat line into one company as envisioned earlier.[81]

That goal apparently could not be achieved, and on October 10, 1904, it was announced that the Queen Anne's Railroad Company and the Queen Anne's Ferry and Equipment Company were to be consolidated with the Chester River Steamboat Company and the Weems Steamboat Company—the oldest on the Bay—into a single corporation known as the Maryland, Delaware and Virginia Railway. It was widely believed at the time that the MD&V was a subsidiary of the Pennsylvania Railroad. The Queen Anne's Railroad Company had been the last independent rail line.

In January 1905, the three steamboat companies and railroad were officially purchased by the MD&V in a foreclosure sale, giving the newly formed company a total of seventeen steamers that would be shifted to various lines over the coming years. All three steamers of the former Queen Anne's Ferry and Equipment Company were sold not long after the amalgamation.

The *Queen Anne* went to Washington buyers who operated her in excursion service on the Potomac River for five years before selling her to a company in Salem, New Jersey, for service on the Delaware River. In 1925, she was sold again to New York interests who renamed her *Rockaway* for operation to the Long Island beach of the same name. In 1930, she was abandoned. The *Queen Caroline* went to New York and was first renamed *Montauk* and later *Transford* and *Ramona*. The Buxton Line, operating between Norfolk and Richmond, Virginia, acquired her in 1929 and brought her back to the Bay to operate on the James River between those two cities as the *Richmond*. She was destroyed by fire on September 30, 1945, while laid up at Claremont, Virginia. The *Endeavor* was sold to the Norfolk and Atlantic Terminal Company for a run between the Norfolk area and Newport News in Hampton Roads. She ran there until 1914, but her ultimate disposition is unknown.

8.

THE BIG BOAT COMES TO THE CHESTER

The largest steamboat to ever operate on the Chester River stayed for only a short time but was known during that period as one of the most comfortable and popular steamers in the Chesapeake Bay region. Her size allowed her to carry thousands of passengers, and she was often packed on her all-too-few trips from Baltimore to the Chester. In the end, her size may have been a factor in her brief time on the river.

The steamer was the *Dreamland*, a side-wheeler of exceptionally neat lines that operated for one season between Baltimore and Queenstown for the Queenstown and Love Point Transportation and Development Company. She was 284 feet long and could carry four thousand passengers. In her heyday, she could do twenty miles an hour, but by the time she arrived on the Chester, her speed was not what it had been in her youth. She was built in 1878 by Harlan and Hollingsworth. There were three passenger decks with considerable open space, two of which stretched the full length of the vessel. Aft on the main deck, the first one above the waterline, was her dining room, surrounded by windows to give diners good views of the passing scenery. There were many who felt she was one of the most beautiful steamboats in America.[82]

Initially named the *Republic*, the steamer was built for Captain Jonathan Cone, owner of Cone's Upper Delaware River Transportation Company, and operated on a daylight run between Philadelphia and Trenton, New Jersey. The *Republic* was the flagship of the fleet and became known as "Queen of the Delaware."[83] She operated on that route from the time of her introduction until about 1900, when Captain Cone sold her to New York interests. She later ran as an excursion boat from Philadelphia to Cape May, New Jersey, and was renamed *Cape May* in 1902. Following that venture, she was acquired by the Dreamland Transportation Company for service between New York City and Coney Island. On June 9, 1904, she was renamed *Dreamland*.[84]

After four years running between New York and Coney Island, the vessel was sold again in 1908. By this time, she was thirty years old, but she had been well built and well maintained—so much so that new owners found a use for her on the Chesapeake Bay and Chester River. She would be operating under the flag of the newly formed Queenstown and Love Point Transportation and Development Company: "The transportation service is intended for general freight and passenger business, but the primary purpose of the enterprise is to popularize the Love Point section, which is regarded as one of the most attractive on the upper bay."[85]

The land at Love Point had been considered earlier as a resort destination by the Queen Anne's Railroad in conjunction with a number of Baltimore investors. Also included were plans for a fairground to be established at Queenstown, including a racetrack, a grandstand, an exhibit hall and stables.[86] But before that could happen, the railroad was absorbed into the Maryland, Delaware and Virginia Railway in 1905. The investors, however, remained interested, and when the venerable *Dreamland* became available, she was purchased to be the transportation link in a proposed new operation.

The entrepreneurs wanted to build a hotel at Love Point and create a resort. They also envisioned Queenstown as a resort-type destination since there was already an amusement park there that had been developed in the late 1890s by the Queenstown Land Development Company. That firm also owned the former Bowlingly estate overlooking Little Queenstown Creek, which was built in the eighteenth century, and had converted it into a hotel for a short time. The Queenstown and Love Point Transportation and Development Company acquired Bowlingly in 1910, reopened it as a hotel and built another long steamboat pier out into Little Queenstown Creek with the hope of attracting excursionists to the area.[87]

The *Dreamland* was brought to Baltimore to undergo renovations, but before she started operating to Love Point and Queenstown, she spent the summer of 1909 making daily excursions from Baltimore down the Bay to Chesapeake Beach, an up-and-coming resort on the Western Shore in Calvert County.

The *Dreamland* at the long dock in Queenstown. The granary and other commercial buildings are at the right. *Courtesy Chesapeake Bay Maritime Museum, H. Graham Wood Collection.*

Finally, in the early summer of 1910, the *Dreamland* was placed on her intended service and quickly proved to be quite popular. The schedule called for departure from Commercial Wharf at the foot of Broadway in Baltimore at 2:45 p.m. daily and at 9:00 a.m. on Sundays. The first stop was Love Point, where embarking passengers could spend four hours before catching the steamer later in the day for the trip back to Baltimore. There was a two-hour layover in Queenstown before the return trip, which arrived back in Baltimore later that evening. While there were many people making it a one-day outing, many others also elected to spend time at the hotels at both locations. Live music, dancing and a variety of amusements were part of the voyage, and the round trip was seventy-five cents.

Large crowds of excursionists from Baltimore and Washington were attracted to the developing resort at Love Point and the park and hotel in Queenstown, but problems quickly developed.

On June 5, the big steamer ran aground in the Chester River near Queenstown with about one hundred people aboard. They had to be removed by a tugboat, which then towed the *Dreamland* off the sandbar. Fortunately, she was undamaged and was able to resume her trips without further delay.

The eighteenth-century Queenstown home known as Bowlingly as it appeared when it was a hotel visited by steamboat passengers. *Author's collection.*

Then, on the evening of July 17, with seven hundred passengers aboard, she grounded once again just three hundred yards from her Queenstown dock and remained stuck for twenty-one hours. For reasons lost to history, it was not possible to take her passengers off, and they were forced to remain on board, many of them sleeping in the main saloon since there were no overnight accommodations.[88] The vessel was refloated at high tide at midafternoon on July 18, again without damage, but when she made her departure from Baltimore the following day, she only went as far as Love Point, leading to speculation that Queenstown would be dropped as a destination.

It was apparent to some that the 284-foot *Dreamland* (which was about 100 feet longer than other Chester River steamers) was too large for the small harbor at Queenstown, although there is no record of any company official actually saying so. The confined harbor was one of the reasons the Queen Anne's Railroad Company had moved its steamer terminal to Love Point earlier. Although it is known that the *Dreamland* made a few more trips to Queenstown that summer, there is no record of any further mishaps.

The *Dreamland* continued, through the summer of 1910, to regularly carry excursionists to Love Point and take on freight and farm products there for Baltimore, but Queenstown is no longer mentioned after mid-July. In fact, no advertising of any part of the service has been found after July 14,

1910. Many Love Point–bound passengers belonged to fraternal and church organizations, which took group trips there for meetings or short vacation stays at the hotel. Passenger loads were quite good for the remainder of the season, but when fall came, the *Dreamland*'s service to Love Point ended.[89]

She was then used for a variety of excursion trips out of Baltimore, but in 1912, the Queenstown and Love Point Transportation and Development Company sold her to new owners who returned her to the Chesapeake Beach run, where she proved quite successful and remained for the next fourteen years. In 1925, at the ripe age of forty-seven, she was laid up and eventually sold for scrap in 1928.

Although the Queenstown and Love Point Transportation and Development Company faded from the scene after the *Dreamland* was sold, the Love Point Hotel and resort remained in operation until 1947, when ferry service ended for good and the hotel closed. It burned under suspicious circumstances in 1965 after standing vacant for many years.

The loss of steamboat excursions that brought fun-seekers to Queenstown, on the other hand, led to the eventual closing of both the amusement park and Bowlingly hotel. The town continued as a port of call for steamers of the Chester River Steamboat Company through 1923, but it was never again a destination for purely pleasure-seeking excursionists.

9.

WAR, ICE, FOG AND STORMS

M ost of the time, voyages between the Chester River and Baltimore took place without incident, the steamers operating with clockwork regularity. But there were times when the Chester River steamers experienced the unexpected—ice, fog, storms and even war.

The War Between the States, as it is sometimes called in Maryland, was less than three months old when a Chester River steamboat unexpectedly found herself in the midst of wartime activity. Sometime during the first week of July 1861, the *Hugh Jenkins*, which was then being operated by Isaac Winchester along with the steamer *Balloon*, departed from Baltimore on what was described as "a secret expedition to Easton" in Talbot County to recover arms believed destined for Southern sympathizers on the Eastern Shore.[90]

A contingent of Federal soldiers went to Easton on the *Hugh Jenkins* but had little success in locating the weapons. According to contemporary accounts, they recovered only a few rifles, but they arrested two people and took them back to Fort McHenry in Baltimore. There being no further mention of the steamer taking part in Union army activities, it appears likely that she returned within a few days to her regular operations.

Next to be temporarily called up was the Slaughter Line flagship *Chester*. Early July found her on her regular route between Crumpton and Baltimore, running in consort with the *Arrow* and calling at many wharves along the way. She was practically brand new and was expected to have a busy but unremarkable life on the route for which she was designed. No one would have dreamed that three months after her maiden voyage, almost to the day, she would be requisitioned by the Federal government for war service.

Then came word that the *Chester* "had been seized at her wharf in Baltimore" by Federal authorities on July 9 for a special mission to the Potomac and Patuxent Rivers that her owners and regular passengers and shippers could never have envisioned.[91]

A Confederate adventurer named Richard Thomas Zarvona had conceived a plan to seize the Federal steamer *St. Nicholas*, which was then on a regular run from Baltimore down Chesapeake Bay and up the Potomac River to Georgetown, near Washington. The seizing of the *St. Nicholas* was part of a grander plan to eventually capture the U.S. Navy gunboat *Pawnee*, to which the *St. Nicholas* often carried supplies. At the time, the *Pawnee* patrolled the portion of the Bay between the Potomac and Patuxent Rivers looking for Confederate blockade runners. By seizing the *St. Nicholas*, Zarvona could then use her to deceive the *Pawnee* and quickly capture her.

Zarvona, along with several compatriots, boarded the *St. Nicholas* in Baltimore on June 28 and took her over shortly after she had made a stop at Point Lookout at the mouth of the Potomac River. She was taken to the Virginia side of the Potomac, where it was learned that the seizure of the *Pawnee* could not take place because she had been recalled from her patrol. Instead, Zarvona took the *St. Nicholas* up the Rappahannock River, where she captured three freight-carrying vessels.

Once Federal officials learned of the incident, Provost Marshal John Kenly in Baltimore ordered the requisitioning of the *Chester* at her Light Street pier early on the morning of July 9 as she was preparing to depart for Chestertown and Crumpton. In short order, her passengers were sent ashore, and in their place a group of eighty armed troops from Massachusetts and Pennsylvania stationed at Fort McHenry came aboard with two twenty-pound guns and a determination to hunt down Zarvona.[92] The *Chester* headed down the Bay looking for any sign of the *St. Nicholas* and her captors, but the crew was unsuccessful and headed back to Baltimore.

The record is unclear on how soon the *Chester* resumed her normal run after her brief fling with military service, but it is assumed she did so within a matter of days. As for Zarvona, he made an attempt to seize another steamer soon after on the Potomac River, but the Federal authorities had been tipped off and he was arrested.

Just weeks before being commandeered, the *Chester* had a different kind of brief encounter with military matters. On June 25, she ran a special charter for the Sabbath School of Chestertown's Methodist Protestant Church to

Annapolis to witness the regimental drill there and see the encampments of the Union forces stationed in the city. The Kennedyville Brass Band provided music for the excursion.

In May 1862, the Chester River steamboat *Balloon* was pressed into service to take a contingent of Federal troops to Easton, where they took into custody Judge Richard Bennett Carmichael, who had publicly taken issue with the arrest by Federal authorities of people considered to be disloyal to the Union following the election of 1861. Carmichael was hearing a case when the soldiers entered his courtroom, grabbed him by the beard and beat him before taking him to the *Balloon*, which was tied up at nearby Wye Landing. An attorney who had tried to help the judge was also taken into custody. Both were taken aboard the steamer to Fort McHenry, where they were imprisoned, but were never formally charged with any crime. A year later, the same vessel took troops to Easton, where Federal authorities arrested the editor of the *Easton Star* for pro-Southern publications. In this case, the arrest was said to have been ordered directly by President Lincoln.[93] The *Balloon* also transported local members of the Second Eastern Shore Militia from Kent County to Pungoteague on Virginia's Eastern Shore for war duty in early 1862. The soldiers had organized at Camp Vickers outside Chestertown.[94]

Although the War Between the States had been over for twenty-three years, the Chester River Steamboat Company steamer *Corsica* found herself involved in a harrowing incident in a different kind of war in 1888. In the mid-nineteenth century, a shooting war developed on the Chesapeake Bay over oyster harvesting between local watermen and New Englanders who came south to take advantage of what then seemed to be an endless supply of the tasty bivalves. Maryland and Virginia watermen wanted the interlopers to go home and leave the Bay's riches for them to harvest. Then the Maryland and Virginia watermen squabbled among themselves over dredging rights and exchanged shots. That was followed by exchanges of gunfire between the watermen of various counties, and by 1868, the situation had become so tense that Maryland was compelled to create the Oyster Navy to try to keep the situation under control.

On the night of December 8, 1888, the *Corsica* was bound down the Chester headed for Baltimore on what everyone expected would be a routine voyage. But it turned out to be anything but. In the darkness near the mouth of the river off Wickes' Beach, the steamer was passing a large fleet of anchored oyster-dredging vessels when some of the men on the smaller boats began yelling at the *Corsica*, prompting several passengers

The *Corsica*, seen at Spry's Landing, had the misfortune to be fired on in 1888 during the Chesapeake oyster wars. *Courtesy of Kevin Hemstock.*

to yell back, according to an account given later by Captain W.J. Taylor. Shots rang out from the oyster boats in the direction of the steamer, forcing the thirty-two passengers to seek shelter in the forward part of the vessel. Although Taylor said most of the dozen or so shots fell short of the *Corsica*, several did strike the port side of the ship's dining room, but no one was hurt.[95]

The steamer continued on her way to Baltimore without any further difficulty, but that was not the end of the incident. When Governor Elihu Jackson heard what had happened, he ordered the *Governor R.M. McLane*, flagship of the Oyster Navy, to seek out the dredgers responsible for firing on the *Corsica*. On the night of December 10, the *McLane* battled with them near Queenstown for four hours, resulting in the sinking of two oyster boats, the capture of their crews and the capture of a third dredge boat. The firing on the *Corsica* was widely condemned, and the *Sun* editorialized, "It is impossible to conceive a more deliberately mischievous assault."[96] On December 11, George Warfield, president of the Chester River Steamboat Company, wrote to Governor Jackson asking that the state provide sufficient protection for its steamers and reminded the governor that the vessels also carried U.S. mail. In his reply, the governor pledged to do whatever was necessary to avoid another incident. (The partially sunken hull of the *Governor R.M. McLane* is still visible in Baltimore Harbor.)

Many visitors to the Chesapeake Bay country from other parts of the nation are surprised to learn that the Bay and its rivers can freeze, given their location in a rather temperate zone. But there have been many times when ice on the Bay was so thick that vessels became trapped and navigation came to a halt. Ice was particularly severe during the years immediately before and after the turn of the twentieth century.

One of those years was 1899. In February, ice covered much of the open Bay and was especially thick in the tributaries, preventing the steamers from making their regular runs. It became necessary for the icebreaker *Annapolis* to break a path from Love Point to Queenstown. The Chester River Steamboat Company, which had temporarily suspended its runs because of the ice, resumed operations with the *B.S. Ford* finally departing from Baltimore on February 23. The *Endeavor* of the Queen Anne's Railroad also resumed service the same day. But the ice closed in again, and all steamers had to tie up. On March 2, the ice near the mouth of the river was reported to be ten to fourteen inches thick, making it necessary for the *Annapolis* to break a path for the *Corsica* on her way to Chestertown. The *Corsica* followed the sturdy icebreaker into Queenstown Harbor and then spent an hour ramming the ice before reaching her dock.[97] The *Corsica*, with the continued assistance of the *Annapolis*, finally reached Chestertown around 6:00 p.m. after an eleven-hour voyage. Normally, the trip would take about seven hours.

The *Kent News* of January 17, 1903, told how the *B.S. Ford* and *Emma A. Ford* were delayed while trying to navigate the river during an exceptionally cold period when the mercury plummeted to eleven degrees. Upon leaving Chestertown, the *Emma* experienced ice all the way to Love Point, which slowed her progress and delayed her an hour in trying to dock at Queenstown. The *B.S. Ford* was headed for Chestertown from Baltimore the same day and experienced "considerable difficulty" trying to land at Queenstown before giving up after trying to get up the Corsica River to Centreville.[98] She made it to Booker's Wharf and unloaded her freight onto wagons that took it to Centreville.

But it was the winter of 1904–05 that appears to have been the worst. During that year, most of the upper Bay and its tributaries were completely covered with ice. On December 15, 1904, the *Emma A. Ford* encountered solid ice all the way down to Booker's Wharf, according to Captain William Taylor, and fell behind schedule but managed to make all of her landings. But then conditions worsened, forcing steamers on the Chester and other rivers and the upper Bay to remain at their docks for long periods. Needless to say, the lengthy disruptions of service due to ice seriously delayed the shipment of needed freight to both sides of the Bay.

The blizzard of January 24–25, 1905, was described as the worst to ever hit Kent County. News reports told of temperatures dipping to six below zero, ice on the river more than six inches thick, snow drifting twenty feet deep on local rail lines and passengers spending an entire night stranded on a train north of Chestertown. And from that point, it stayed frigid for weeks, and no vessels moved on the river for more than a month. Finally, on Wednesday, March 1, the icebreaker *F.C. Latrobe* from Baltimore succeeded in breaking its way across the Bay as far as Swan Point north of Rock Hall but did not try to go any farther. The next day, the *Gratitude* managed to make it across the Bay to Rock Hall but, because of the thick ice, was not able to make the wharf and turned around. The Chester River Steamboat Company made several attempts to get a boat up the river but didn't succeed until Wednesday, March 8, when the *Gratitude*, with the assistance of an icebreaker, made it to Chestertown. "We have been without a boat since Jan. 25th," the *Kent News* reported on March 11, the same day navigation was again declared open.

If it wasn't ice playing havoc with navigation, it was fog or storms. Squalls on the Chesapeake Bay are notorious for blowing up out of nowhere, raging for twenty minutes to half an hour and then disappearing completely. One such storm caught the *Gratitude* on the open Bay on Monday, April 27, 1896, and she was tossed around by the steep waves. Several small boats were also caught in the storm and at least one capsized, but the *Gratitude* was near and pulled its occupants to safety. There was another storm on August 21, 1899, that made for a difficult voyage for one of the steamers as she headed for Baltimore:

> *The steamer* **B.S. Ford,** *running for the Queen Anne's Ferry, ran into the storm on Monday night last at the mouth of the Chester river and the passengers experienced an unpleasant time for a while. There was a crowd aboard the steamer and during the excitement several women fainted and the officers were kept busy quieting the fears of the passengers. Two heavy seas struck the steamer, washing overboard a quantity of tomatoes stowed on the forward deck, the water entering the enclosed lower deck.* [99]

Then there was the time on an unknown date when the *B.S. Ford* started across the Bay from Baltimore in a nor'easter, prompting a female passenger to ask the captain if it was too risky. "Lady, I think just as much of my life as you do," the captain replied, ending the discussion. [100]

Fog can form on the Bay and rivers with virtually no warning, reduce visibility to near zero and then hang around for a while. One such situation occurred on November 3, 1904, as the *Emma A. Ford* headed for Chestertown. She encountered fog near Love Point, and it got worse as she headed upriver toward Queenstown, forcing the vessel to skip that landing and keep going. But the fog had gotten so thick that her searchlight was unable to penetrate it, so relying on her own whistle and foghorns ashore, she was eventually able to make it to Bogle's Wharf on Eastern Neck Island. She was forced to remain there for thirteen hours before attempting to continue her voyage to Chestertown early the next morning. During that unexpected long layover, sleeping accommodations were somehow found for most of the female passengers, and breakfast was provided at no charge to the twenty-nine passengers. The captain said it was only the second time in forty years that he had been stopped for so long because of fog.

Fortunately, these unexpected disruptions in operation were few, and the majority of the time, it was smooth sailing for the Chester River steamers. In fact, the Chester River Steamboat Company had an impeccable safety record and never lost a passenger over the years.[101]

10.

TWO DECADES OF CHANGE

The period from 1886 through 1905 was one of change and challenge for the Chester River Steamboat Company. It was marked by sporadic competition, acquisition of another company and finally the purchase of the Chester River Steamboat Company by a transportation titan.

In 1886, there were two competing companies: the Enterprise Line, which had been on the scene since 1882, and a new firm simply called the People's Line. The latter was exclusively a freight line that touched at several wharves. It operated the steamer *E.N. Fairchild* in the summer on a route that began at Buckingham Wharf on the upper Chester and included stops at Snitcher's, Chestertown, Burchinal's and Quaker Neck. It operated for only about two summer seasons.

Meanwhile, the Enterprise Line was operating from Pier 12, Light Street in Baltimore, with the propeller-driven steamer *Captain Miller* that succeeded the *Enterprise*, which had earlier been sold. The *Captain Miller* had a varied career that included not only Chesapeake Bay but also the Delaware River, the Mississippi River and the waters around New Orleans. She was built in 1880 in Philadelphia as the *Gratitude* and operated from Philadelphia until 1882, when she was shifted to a run between New Orleans and Pensacola, Florida, and renamed *Captain Miller*. She operated out of Natchez, Tennessee, in 1885 and was sold the following year to the Centreville and Corsica River Steamboat Company, successor to the Enterprise Line, for service between Centreville and Baltimore. On that route, she called at Long Cove and Jackson Creek near Kent Island.

In 1886, the steamer *Gratitude*, formerly the *Captain Miller*, began operating on the Chester River. A landing in Rock Hall was named for it. *The Mariners' Museum, Newport News, Virginia.*

Disaster caught up with the *Captain Miller* on April 23, 1887, when she caught fire at her wharf in Centreville. She was tied up for the night when the ship's cook discovered the blaze shortly after 3:30 a.m., forcing members of the crew to just barely escape before the vessel's wooden upper works were consumed by flames. She burned so fiercely that the freight shed on the wharf nearly caught fire. The schooner *Chesterfield*, lying nearby, was also briefly in danger, but she was moved before the fire could reach her. When her mooring lines burned through, the *Captain Miller* drifted to the far shore of the Corsica River, by which time all that was left was the iron hull and her machinery.[102]

Fortunately, the hull and engines were in good condition despite the intense heat, and it was decided to rebuild and lengthen the steamer and once again name her *Gratitude*. She returned to her Chester River run and was still there when the Chester River Steamboat Company purchased the Centreville and Corsica River Steamboat Company in 1890. At that point, the *Gratitude* was shifted to a route between Rock Hall and Baltimore and, in the process, wound up having a wharf named after her.[103] She became such a favorite that local residents named the area of Rock Hall near where Swan Creek meets the Bay in her honor, a name that has stuck to the present. There is currently a Gratitude Marina there, which has an image of the steamer on the sign at its entrance.

It was during the late 1880s that the Chester River Steamboat Company built a large wharf at Rock Hall. Prior to that, passengers from the Rock Hall area had to catch the boat at Grey's Inn landing, which made for a four-hour trip to Baltimore. Departure directly from Rock Hall reduced the travel time to two hours and "will be a great convenience to a large class of people and probably draw off many who now go to the city by way of Tolchester."[104]

The freight business, particularly the shipment of peaches, was booming leading into the last decade of the nineteenth century. The year 1888 was especially a banner year when experts estimated that peach farms on the Delmarva Peninsula were expected to produce between eight and ten million baskets of the fruit. All steamboat companies serving the Eastern Shore carried record amounts that year, but the Chester River Steamboat Company was said to have handled more than any other. There were those

Rock Hall, on the Chesapeake Bay, was the last landing for steamboats bound for Baltimore from Chester River points. *Courtesy Chesapeake Bay Maritime Museum, H. Graham Wood Collection.*

who reported seeing baskets of peaches stacked all the way to the overhead on the freight decks of most steamers. The company built or expanded existing wharves on the river as well as its pier in Baltimore to expedite the shipment of peaches:

> *The total carrying capacity of the* [Chester River] *boats will be 45,000 baskets per day. Tugs and lighters will ply up the tributaries of the Chester river, and will transfer their cargoes to the river steamers, which will make a trip each day to Baltimore, the first arriving at 1 A.M. and the others following in quick succession, except the* Emma A. Ford *and the* B.S. Ford, *which will arrive in the afternoon.*[105]

Wheat, corn and oats, along with peaches and tomatoes, were shipped in large quantities from the Eastern Shore. Also filling the freight decks of the westbound steamers were such commodities as oyster shells, salt, fish, oysters, poultry, bacon, sheep, cattle and mules. Freight bound for the Eastern Shore included coal, lumber, shingles, laths, square timber, bricks, lime, tools, farm equipment and general merchandise.

In correspondence with the U.S. Army Corps of Engineers over dredging of upper portions of the Chester River, company president George Warfield provided statistics on the company's freight operations. For 1895, he wrote, the company shipped from Crumpton alone 1,128 tons of fruit, tomatoes and similar crops and 2,670 tons of corn, wheat and other grains from the Eastern Shore to Baltimore. By comparison, from Baltimore to Crumpton, it transported 462 tons of fertilizers and 427 tons of general merchandise.[106] That was just for one port, and the numbers for many of the other wharves along the river were likely similar during the same period. An example of the size of some of these shipments can be gleaned from a brief item in the *Kent News* of September 28, 1889, which stated that the *Emma A. Ford* "landed four tons of phosphate on a section of the wharf and it gave way precipitating all upon it into the river."[107] Although people got wet and dirty, there was no report of any injuries.

In June 1889, there was sufficient freight and passenger business to keep three of its four steamers operating on a daily basis except for Sunday, each from a different port, during the growing season. The *Emma A. Ford* ran from Chestertown, the *B.S. Ford* ran from Centreville and the *Corsica* ran from Crumpton. Those who maintained the ledgers of the Chester River Steamboat Company must have been very happy, indeed.

But then, the bottom fell out.

Once a daily scene, the *Emma A. Ford* passes a schooner as it steams up the Chester River. *Courtesy of the Mark Newsome collection.*

During the winter months, the Chester River Steamboat Company often cut its daily operations to every other day from Chestertown and Centreville. *Author's collection.*

THE WINTER SCHEDULE
—OF THE—
Chester River Steamboat Company
Monday, November 17th, 1902.

Str. B. S. Ford | Emma A. Ford

Leave Centreville...............7 A. M. Tuesdays, Thursdays and Saturdays, stopping at landings on Corsica River, Queenstown, Jackson's Creek Kent Island and Rock Hall..	Leave Chestertown..... ....8 A. M. Mondays, Wednesdays and Fridays, Stopping at Rolph's, Bookers, Quaker Neck, Cliffs, Bogles, Queenstown and Kent Island.
Leave Baltimore.......... .11.00 A. M. Mondays, Wednesdays and Fridays, stopping at Rock Hall, Kent Island, and Jackson's Creek, Queenstown and landings on Corsica River.	Leave Baltimore............11.00 A. M. Tuesdays, Thursdays and Saturdays, stopping at Kent Island, Queenstown, Bogles, Cliffs, Quaker Neck, Booker's, Rolph's and Chestertown.

Saturday Afternoon Trips to and from Rock Hall.
Steamer B. S. Ford will leave Baltimore at 3.00 P. M.; Rock Hall, 5.15 P. M

GEORGE WARFIELD, President.
JAMES E. TAYLOR, General Agent.

A major peach blight hit the Delmarva Peninsula in the early 1890s, decimating what had been a thriving industry. It was a disease known as the "peach yellows," and it struck practically every orchard in Maryland and Delaware. The disease was caused by a group of organisms "similar to viruses but with characteristics of bacteria as well. It is endemic to the eastern U.S."[108] The peach yellows did their worst between 1890 and 1900.[109] Although a few orchards remain on the Eastern Shore today, the peach crop never rebounded to the levels it experienced in the late 1800s. Other crops and farm products continued to be carried on the Chester River steamers, but it just wasn't the same. Added to this devastating development was the increased presence of railroads on the Eastern Shore.

Railroads first appeared on the shore in 1830, when the New Castle and Frenchtown Turnpike and Railroad Company began operating in Cecil County and Delaware. It was slow going for many efforts to build railroads on the shore, but eventually, more lines were created that could link up with much larger railroads, such as the mighty Pennsylvania Railroad, which had been chartered in 1846 and immediately began to grow. Local roads included the Queen Anne's and Kent Railroad; the Maryland and Delaware Railroad; and the Delaware, Maryland and Virginia Railroad. It was 1872 before a rail line made it to Chestertown. Many of the smaller lines were eventually taken over by the Pennsylvania Railroad as it extended its reach.[110] Over time, the rail lines began to spread into parts of the Eastern Shore that had once been the purview of the steamboat, creating a competitive atmosphere between the two modes of transportation. Eventually, the Chester River Steamboat Company felt the presence of the railroads as some freight previously handled by the steamers shifted to the railroads for shipment to Philadelphia instead of Baltimore.

During the 1890s, however, it remained pretty much business as usual, although the precipitous decline in the number of peaches carried during that decade was a major concern. That period saw the steamers also running a considerable number of special trips in the summer. There were excursions from the Chester River to the resort of Bay Ridge near Annapolis and visits to the state capital itself. Many of these special trips were on the *B.S. Ford*. One somewhat unusual excursion was a church Sunday school trip down the river, past Rock Hall to the amusement park at Tolchester Beach which, in terms of miles, was a relatively short overland trip. But of course, the opportunity to spend several hours on a beautiful steamboat was a strong draw.

Pier 7, Light Street, was always bustling with activity when a steamer arrived or departed. The *Emma A. Ford* is alongside the dock. *Courtesy of Steve Frohock.*

An unusual view of the *B.S. Ford* in Baltimore's Fells Point, apparently during a charter or excursion trip. *Courtesy of the Mark Newsome collection.*

Most of the steamboat lines on the Chesapeake Bay were independently owned and operated and were the main means of transporting passengers and freight up and down and across the Bay and its tributaries.

But not for long: "The Pennsylvania Railroad disliked the competition to its Eastern Shore rail lines from independent steamboat lines that operated from Baltimore to various shore points. It therefore worked incognito to acquire as many of these lines as possible."[111]

A complicated series of transactions began in 1894 that saw the sale of the Choptank Steamboat Company, the Eastern Shore Steamboat Company and the Maryland Steamboat Company to the Eastern Shore Railroad, which was reorganized as the Baltimore, Chesapeake and Atlantic Railway Company—a subsidiary of the Pennsylvania Railroad. In the process, the railroad became the owner of fifteen steamers and their wharves on several major rivers. The routes it controlled were the Baltimore-Claiborne Ferry, the Choptank River Line, Nanticoke River Line, Occohannock River Line, Pocomoke River Line, Piankatank River Line, Tuckahoe River Line, Wicomico River Line and the Great Wicomico River Line that altogether represented 118 wharves and 1,134 miles of steamer lines.[112] This would not, however, be the last steamboat line takeover by companies affiliated with the Pennsylvania.

In the summer of 1896, an unidentified steamboat company was reported to be planning permanent passenger and freight operations on the Chester River at low rates. Although the name of the company has not survived, the mere idea of another steamboat line was rejected in the local media, which was quick to sing the praises of the Chester River Steamboat Company:

> *That company has a well established line, splendid steamers, polite and capable officers, low fares, and everything the public could ask at its hands in any degree of business. It has friends, who will stand by it, and who will discourage any more of the pop opposition lines that have so often deceived the people here with their pretended permanency and better service. The people here feel that they had better by far have one good boat and efficient services, rather than two or three half companies with small boats, uncertain rates [and] temporary accommodations.*[113]

And that was that. The proposed newcomer was never heard from again.

The first public indication that the Chester River Steamboat Company might be in the takeover sights of the railroads surfaced in December 1899, when it was learned that the Wheeler Line, a company operating between

Baltimore and Hillsboro on the Tuckahoe River, was to be purchased by the Pennsylvania. Rumors were rampant at the time that the Chester River Steamboat Company might be next, but a company official quickly sought to quash that speculation:

> *I have not been approached by any representative of the Pennsylvania Railroad Company in reference to the sale of this property. The only information we have is what we have heard on the streets and seen in the newspapers, and until some proposition is made we are not in a position to discuss the matter.*[114]

A little more than three years later, however, the situation appears to have changed, judging by an entry in the minutes of the Chester River Steamboat Company board of directors. The minutes show that on April 17, 1902, there was brief discussion on a resolution to authorize the board to sell all of the company's stock and property.[115] That resolution does not appear to have been acted on.

The speculation, however, finally came to an end on October 10, 1904, when it was announced in Baltimore that the Chester River Steamboat Company, the Queen Anne's Railroad Company and the Weems Steamboat Company (the oldest on the Bay) had been sold. The sale was to "a syndicate of New York, Philadelphia, and Wilmington capitalists" for a reported $2.5 million, and "the impression prevails that the purchase is being made in the interest of the Pennsylvania Railroad, which, according to rumor, will ultimately acquire absolute control."[116]

It didn't take long for change to occur. On November 1, 1904, three of the directors of the Chester River Steamboat Company, including President George Warfield, resigned. Warfield's place was taken by Willard Thomson, vice-president and general manager of the Baltimore, Chesapeake and Atlantic Railway. Other BC&A officials took the other directors' posts. The Queen Anne Railroad Company's Baltimore–Love Point–Cape May service was terminated, and its traffic was moved to an all-rail route to Philadelphia.[117] These developments were followed on January 30, 1905, by the incorporation of the Maryland, Delaware and Virginia Railway Company—a Pennsylvania Railroad subsidiary—which would manage steamboat operations on the Chester and those that had been maintained by the Weems Line. Including the various routes of the Weems Line and the Chester River Steamboat Company, the MD&V had 979 miles of water routes and 144 wharves.[118] By the time all was said and done, the

A receipt for the shipment of freight aboard a steamer on the Maryland, Delaware and Virginia Railway's Chester River Line. *Author's collection.*

Pennsylvania Railroad, through its subsidiaries, owned nearly all steamboat lines on the Bay north of the York River in Virginia.[119]

Initially, the name Chester River Steamboat Company was retained, but the operation would eventually come to be known as the Chester River Line of the MD&V. The spring of 1905 saw the retirement of the popular Captain P.S. McConnor after forty consecutive years on the river. He was considered to be one of the best pilots taking steamers in and out of Baltimore. Also that spring, advertisements appeared for another steamboat company, this one a freight-only operation using what was only described as an able vessel. This short-lived operation, as opposed to the many other earlier ones that had been based in Baltimore or Chestertown, was headquartered in Queenstown. A company called the Steam Freight Line, operating between Baltimore, Rock Hall and Centreville with the powerboat *Lauretta Curran* three days a week, appeared in May 1906, but as with most of the others, it lasted only a short time.

In October 1906, there was a rare occurrence—a strike by steamboat captains, and the first master to walk off his vessel was Captain William Taylor of the *B.S. Ford*. The captains of the MD&V and the BC&A asked for a pay increase of about 50 percent, feeling it justified, given the demands of their jobs and the fact that they were often away from their families. When the request was not granted, they and their officers tied up their boats and refused to take them out. The strike certainly didn't do the companies' ledger books any good as freight piled up on the wharves and passengers looked to other modes of transportation. Finally, an arbitration committee found in favor of the captains, and they were granted a raise, ending the strike on October 13 after thirteen days.[120]

The vessels of the Chester River Steamboat Company continued to steam on, but times were changing for steamboats.

11.

THE TWILIGHT YEARS

As the first decade of the twentieth century unfolded, the transportation landscape was changing. Rail lines branched out farther across the Eastern Shore, economical gasoline engine–powered boats were taking away some of the waterborne commerce and roads were improving every day, allowing trucks access to more and more markets. There were factors mitigating against the steamboats during this period, including harsh winter weather that tied up boats for extended periods, the continuing decline in the peach output, less-than-outstanding seasons for the pea crop and a decline in the shipment of oysters and canned goods. There were significant crop declines in 1905 and 1906, and the steamers' freight decks were often at considerably less than capacity. Another factor was that in 1906, the U.S. Post Office cut back the amount of mail moved by steamboat in favor of other methods of transportation. Shipment of mails had been a lucrative business since the very earliest days of steamers on Chesapeake Bay.

There were also costly new safety measures mandated by the federal government following the fire in 1904 that destroyed the steamboat *General Slocum* and killed 1,021 people in New York Harbor. Maintenance costs for vessels, wharves and buildings increased as those properties grew older, and crew wages increased on a regular basis.[121] The parent MD&V system also suffered a major financial setback when its steamer *St. Mary's* was destroyed by fire in the Patuxent River in December 1907.

Fire was the one thing that steamboat operators feared the most because all steamers had wooden superstructures. If a fire could not be contained early, there was a good chance the vessel would not be saved. In 1906, the *Emma A. Ford* was damaged in a fire but was able to be rebuilt. During repairs, her forward deck was enclosed as it had been on the *B.S. Ford*. She was renamed *Love Point* and placed on the Baltimore–Love Point run in April 1906. The *B.S. Ford, Corsica* and *Gratitude* continued providing service from Chestertown and Centreville, but it was not always on a daily basis.

All of this is not meant to suggest that the steamboat industry suddenly fell on hard times to the point where quality of service was reduced or vessels were in disrepair. Changes had been gradually taking place, and for the first time in their long history, the steamers were confronting challenges on several fronts. The financial stability of the Chester River Line began fluctuating, causing concern at company offices. For instance, at the end of 1908, the company reported a decrease in gross earnings of $16,471, which represented a deficit, apparently for the first time.[122] However, there was a turnaround the following year when gross revenues were up $39,191, and the company was sufficiently encouraged to build a new wharf at Cliffs City and order construction of the steamer *Three Rivers* for its Potomac River route. Funding for the *Three Rivers* was made

The steamer *Love Point*, the former *Emma A. Ford*, at Love Point in 1909. *Courtesy of the Mark Newsome collection.*

The *Love Point*, ex–*Emma A. Ford*, in Baltimore's Inner Harbor. *Henry F. Rinn photograph, author's collection.*

possible, in part, by insurance settlements from the burning of the *St. Mary's*. Another setback was the destruction by fire of the *Love Point* on March 11, 1909.

In the second fire of her career, the former *Emma A. Ford* was destroyed at her dock at Love Point when, fortunately, no passengers were aboard. The blaze broke out around 9:45 p.m. when only the crew members were on board. "Every effort was made to extinguish the fire, but the steamer was destroyed. No loss of life and no person was injured. Estimated loss, $90,000," the official report stated ever so briefly.[123] To replace the *Love Point* on the Baltimore–Love Point run, the company brought in the steamer *Westmoreland*, which operated on the route for a number of years.

Company reports from 1910 through 1913 spoke of revenue increases, but after 1913, unprofitability returned and became the norm through most of the second decade of the twentieth century. The number of paved roads on the Eastern Shore continued to increase, making it much easier for trucks and private automobiles to reach areas once served only by steamboats. Passenger numbers were off, and the financial picture wasn't helped any by heavy damage to some of the company's wharves by ice in the winter of 1912. It also sold some land it owned in Chestertown in an effort to improve the financial situation.[124] As if all of these developments weren't enough, the *Gratitude* was sunk in a collision in April 1914 while on the Baltimore–Claiborne run of the affiliated BC&A.

She was arriving at Claiborne as the steamer *Cambridge* was leaving the dock, but because of a misunderstanding in signals, the *Cambridge* plowed into the port side of the *Gratitude*, leaving a gaping hole. She settled in about twelve feet of water, and the *Cambridge* was beached to prevent her from also sinking. There were only a few passengers on each boat, and they were rescued without incident.[125] The *Gratitude* was eventually raised and repaired but was sold in October 1914 to the Bennett Line for operation between Norfolk, Virginia, and North Carolina landings. Later, she ran on the Potomac River out of Washington, D.C., until being sold in 1926 and renamed *Cuba* for service around that island nation.

Loss of the *Gratitude* left the MD&V's Chester River Line with the *B.S. Ford* and the *Corsica* between Chestertown, Crumpton and Baltimore. By then, a number of the wharves that had once been part of the regular schedule were visited by the steamers only on signal. It was interesting to note that a booklet published by the MD&V and BC&A in 1915 about their various lines said of the Chester River Line that "as sailings on this line are somewhat uncertain at this time, those anticipating such a trip should make inquiry later in the season."[126] That might seem to suggest that management was giving thought to giving up the Chester River Line, but as things turned out, it soldiered on for several more years.

In 1909, the *Love Point* was destroyed by fire at its Love Point dock. *Courtesy of Ann Ervin.*

There was no decline in the quality of service, however. The two remaining boats were maintained in top condition, both mechanically and in terms of their onboard amenities, and ran on schedule. An outing on a Chester River Line steamer still made for a good trip.

In 1916, the company's deficit had risen to $132,056. At the same time, maintenance costs of steamboats, wharves, railroad rolling stock, track and bridges also rose, and by the end of that year, the company informed its stockholders that increased rates might be required to help offset the losses. Then in 1917, the United States entered World War I, a move that impacted the Chester River Line as well as most other American steamboat and railroad lines. The federal government took control of all those lines as of January 1, 1918, to be managed by the Federal Railroad Administration for the duration of hostilities in an effort to provide a unified operation. Despite the attempt at streamlined operations, upkeep on steamers and rail equipment all over the nation suffered, even though most vessels were still manned by their peacetime crews, much to the consternation of the various steamboat and railroad lines.[127] During the period of federal operation, the Chester River Line removed the freight shed from the Queenstown dock, apparently as an economy measure.

Although the war ended in 1918, the government retained control of the transportation lines until March 1, 1920, when it returned the boats and trains to their owners. Financial concerns continued to dog the line, and the red ink ran freely. It had reached the point that the company was unable to pay coupons on its mortgage bonds. "It is evident that the continued operation of several of the railway and boat lines cannot be continued with the expectation of making a profit," MD&V stockholders were told that year.[128] In concluding his pessimistic report for 1920, company president Turnbull Murdoch stated, "The Company cannot escape facing a serious financial reorganization."[129] The boats carried on, but the end was in sight.

The financial well finally ran dry, and on May 7, 1923, the MD&V was offered for sale, broken down into three separate parcels. One of those parcels included the Chester River Line, the Patuxent River Line and the steamers *B.S. Ford*, *Corsica* and *Westmoreland* to be sold to Pennsylvania interests described in the local press as "Philadelphia junk dealers."[130] There was concern aplenty in Kent and Queen Anne's Counties that the era of steamboat transportation on the Chester River was coming to an end after more than a century.

During the remainder of 1923, the line was operated by Noel W. Smith, a vice-president of the Pennsylvania Railroad.[131] Despite a flurry of hopeful reports that steamer service might yet be continued, the end came swiftly. It was announced on December 22, 1923, that steamboat service on the Chester "will until further notice cease after Sunday, December 30th 1923" and that "the last trip of a steamer to points above Queenstown, Cliffs to Chestertown, inc., will be on Thursday, December 27th, 1923."[132] Unfortunately, there would no "further notice."

Quietly, and without fanfare, the steamers made their last runs, and for the first time since 1821, the atmosphere lacked the steam whistle announcing the boat's arrival at the dock, the anticipation of passengers waiting on a country wharf, livestock being pushed bodily aboard vessels or elegant meals served in a cheerful dining room.

Important Notice!

CHESTER RIVER LINE

The steamboat service now operated on the Chester River Line by the Maryland, Delaware and Virginia Railway Company (as agent for owners) will until further notice cease after Sunday, December 30th 1923.

The last trip of steamer to points above Queenstown, Cliffs to Chestertown, inc., will be on Thursday, December 27th, 1923.

R. H. SOULSBY,
General Frt. & Pass. Agent

A small newspaper notice published on December 22, 1923, constituted the obituary notice for the MD&V's Chester River Line. The steamers never ran on the river again. *From the* Kent News.

The Chester River Line wasn't the only one to come to an end with the bankruptcy and breakup of the MD&V. Also being abandoned was rail service to Lewes and Rehoboth and the steamer service to Claiborne that connected with the rail line to Ocean City. Instead, the steamer *Cambridge* was placed on the Baltimore to Love Point route, which became the new transfer point for trains headed to Ocean City. In 1931, the Pennsylvania Railroad subsidiary Baltimore and Eastern Railroad began a passenger and auto ferry from Baltimore to Love Point. The vessel chosen was the double-ended ferry *Philadelphia*, best known locally as "Smokey Joe" for the clouds of black coal smoke she generated. A local favorite, she continued to carry passengers and their cars until the line was abandoned on August 31, 1947. The Nanticoke River route was also soon abandoned, and service to the Patuxent River was cut back significantly.

The *B.S. Ford* went to the BC&A for use on various lines and remained on the Chesapeake, and the *Corsica* was sold to new owners in New York and was put on a Long Island run. She continued in that role until the 1930s and was apparently abandoned in 1938. Although the *Ford* was by then forty-six years old, she still had a lot of life left in her in various guises. In 1927, it was the BC&A's turn to be broken up in a foreclosure sale of several parcels. The *Ford* was part of a parcel that included all BC&A wharves and ten other steamers that went to the Baltimore and Virginia Steamboat Company, yet another Pennsylvania Railroad subsidiary. She remained with the Baltimore and Virginia until 1929, when she was sold to Captain George F. Curlett.

A native of Queen Anne's County who grew up near Booker's Wharf, Curlett had a long-standing love affair with the *Ford* and vowed as a youngster to someday be her captain. He worked on various steamers and, in the late 1920s, got involved in carrying Chesapeake Bay freight on powerboats at a time when many steamboats were being retired. He came up with the idea of obtaining a steamer and converting it into a powerboat larger than any others, and no other boat but his old flame, the *B.S. Ford*, would do. She became available when the Baltimore and Virginia Steamboat Company started selling off its steamers, and he bought her in May 1929. Eager to show off his new acquisition, he told his father to be at Love Point at a specific time, and he went steaming proudly by in his favorite steamer. He was not only her captain but also her owner.[133]

Curlett decided to convert the old side-wheeler into a diesel-powered propeller freighter for use on the Bay and had her towed to Norfolk, Virginia, in November 1929 to have the work done. Things did not start off well, however. On her first trial run as a powerboat, her engine was ruined because of a mistake on the part of her engineer, so she returned to the shipyard to have another engine installed. Her first voyage as a freighter was in November 1930 to Havre de Grace, where she loaded stone for a State Roads Commission construction project on the Patuxent River.[134] One might have thought at the time that she would settle down into a routine and continue as a freighter for a few more years before being sold for scrap, given her age. But more adventures lay ahead for the venerable former side-wheeler.

In October 1934, word reached Baltimore that while on a voyage carrying lumber between North Carolina and Baltimore, the *Ford* had collided with the *Kitty Woodall*, another small inland water freighter based in Baltimore. The collision occurred in the Alligator–Pungo Canal in North Carolina, and the *Woodall* sank in the shallow water. No one was injured, and the cause of the accident was not clear. The *Ford* was able to return to Baltimore for repairs. The *Woodall*, owned by the Norfolk, Baltimore and Carolina Line, was raised and returned to service.[135] However, a more serious accident was soon to follow.

On June 7, 1936, as she was making her way across Hampton Roads, Virginia, with a cargo of lumber bound from New Bern, North Carolina, to Baltimore, the *B.S. Ford* was rammed and sunk near Old Point Comfort by the Norfolk and Washington Steamboat Company's overnight passenger and freight steamer *District of Columbia*. Captain Curlett and his crew of eight reached shore safely in lifeboats. The *District of Columbia* was not seriously damaged and continued on her trip to Washington.[136]

Undaunted, Captain Curlett had his boat raised but decided she had not had much luck as a freighter, so he converted her into a lumber-carrying barge to be towed between Baltimore and North Carolina ports by his diesel-powered yacht *Dixie*. In that incarnation, her superstructure was removed down to the main (or freight) deck, and the wheelhouse was moved to the stern to provide accommodations for her riding crew. It was said that the *Ford* could carry 250,000 feet of lumber on her deck and in her hold. The successful conversion of the old steamer into a profitable barge prompted Captain Curlett to buy up other retired steamers and convert them to barges as well. It was a business that prospered well past the halfway point of the twentieth century.

The end for the *B.S. Ford* finally came on October 23, 1960, when, as she was being towed into the Honga River near Hooper Island with a cargo of grain, she ran aground, sank and was a total loss. Her career of eighty-

The *B.S. Ford* briefly became a freighter and then was cut down to a barge carrying lumber, a role in which she continued until 1960. *Photograph by Robert H. Burgess, from the collection of R. Bruce Burgess.*

three years as a steamboat, diesel freighter and barge was unmatched by any other Chesapeake Bay steamer. Perhaps some of her remains still exist in the shallows of the Honga River.

Years after the Chester River Line ceased operations, two steamboats did visit the Chester River but only on a few occasions. The side-wheeler *Emma Giles*, best known for her trips to Tolchester, did a series of all-day excursions from Baltimore to Chestertown on Fridays in the summer of 1932:

> *Unlike her predecessors, she steamed right by the wharves along the bank, most of them decaying in 1932. Instead, loaded with picnickers, she cruised along at a stately gait, headed for the point where a bridge half a mile long crossed the river and the small colonial city of Chestertown graced the left bank.*[137]

But the *Emma Giles*, built in 1887, had seen better days, "and her appearance showed it."[138] At the end of the summer of 1932, Tolchester Line officials realized they could not make the kind of profits needed to keep the boat running, and she never returned to the Chester River. She was converted to a barge four years later.

After the end of the Chester River Line, only an occasional steamer visited the river. One of them was the famous *Emma Giles* in the 1930s. *Courtesy of Robert J. Lewis.*

The *Bay Belle* was the last steamer to visit the Chester River. She ran several excursions in the 1950s. *Author's collection.*

The last time a steamboat came up the river to Chestertown was in the 1950s, when the Wilson Line steamer *Bay Belle* made several special excursions before and after her regular season of running between Baltimore and Betterton. These were few and far between, however, and came to an end in the mid-1950s, less than a decade before the *Bay Belle* ended her career on the Chesapeake.

The boats and landings are now long gone with the exception of Indiantown Wharf, which has been described as the only one still in existence. Repaired and revised over the years, it maintains its original footprint. Occasionally at extreme low tide, the remains of the Crumpton Wharf poke above the surface, and there is a piling or two at other locations. Reminders of that bygone age live on in the form of road signs—Rolph's Wharf Road, Bogles Wharf Road, Steamboat Avenue and Old Wharf Lane in Queenstown and Old Steam Ship Road on Kent Island.

Fortunately, the Chester River looks today much as it did in the heyday of the steamboats, and it is not difficult to glance downriver and imagine the *B.S. Ford* or the *Emma A. Ford* rounding the point above Rolph's Wharf headed for Chestertown, her whistle sounding her imminent arrival.

What times those must have been.

The Indiantown Wharf on the Chester River as it appears today. *Author's photograph.*

A number of roads with names held over from the steamboat era serve as reminders of that period. *Author's photograph.*

The remains of what is believed to be the Crumpton steamboat wharf can occasionally be seen in the shallows at low tide. *Author's photograph.*

Rolph's Wharf today has a marina, a beach, a restaurant and the former boardinghouse now known as the River Inn. *Author's photograph.*

Gratitude Marina in Rock Hall, named for the steamboat *Gratitude*, features a likeness of it in its sign at its entrance. *Author's photograph.*

The former Queen Anne's Railroad Company trestle over Tuckahoe Creek in the town of Queen Anne still stands as a reminder of a bygone era. *Author's photograph.*

To Kentland's Green Garden
By Folger McKinsey

Over the bay on the B.S. *Ford,*
over the bay to the garden of the Lord
Planted in Kentland with beauty and gleam
Of meadows and orchards in mirrors of dream—
Rock Hall and Queenstown and Bogles and Cliffs,
And then the green wheat, and the in between whiffs
Of locust and honey—my heart is a sailor,
Over the bay with my friend, Captain Taylor.
Ho! Her cut-water
Away on the Ford
To Kentland's green garden,
The dream of the Lord![139]

STEAMBOATS KNOWN TO HAVE OPERATED ON THE CHESTER RIVER

U.S. Government Official Number (ON) follows vessel's name when known. Place of construction, dimensions and disposition included when known. Data compiled from various editions of Merchant Vessels of the United States *and the* Lytle Holdcamper List of Merchant Steam Vessels of the United States, 1790–1868.

Arrow ON 88, built 1855, New Castle, Delaware; 123 gross tons; abandoned 1883.

Balloon ON 2032, built 1834, New York; 204 gross tons; acquired by the U.S. Quartermaster Division on September 9, 1861; re-documented on March 9, 1866; burned at Kaighns Point, New Jersey, on October 29, 1872.

Bay Belle ON 207202, built 1910, Wilmington, Delaware; 663 gross tons, 201 feet long, 46 feet wide; originally named *City of Wilmington*; sunk at Boston, Massachusetts, circa 1990.

Boston, built 1831, New York, New York; 380 gross tons; abandoned 1857.

B.S. Ford ON 3045, built 1877, Wilmington, Delaware; 164 feet long, 27 feet wide, 417 gross tons; built for Chester River Steamboat Company; converted to diesel freighter in 1935; converted to unpowered barge in 1936; ran aground and sank in the Honga River, Maryland, on October 23, 1960.

Cambridge, built 1846, Baltimore, Maryland; 462 gross tons; burned at Carter's Creek, Virginia, on September 16, 1853.

Cecil ON 21451, built 1849, Baltimore, Maryland; 117 gross tons; sold to the U.S. Quartermaster Department on June 30, 1863, for government use and re-documented May 19, 1866, as *Rockaway*; lost 1878.

Chesapeake, built 1834, Washington, D.C.; 234 gross tons; abandoned 1854.

Chester ON 4049, built 1861, Chestertown, Maryland; 326 gross tons, 402 horsepower; built for Slaughter Line, transferred to Chester River Steamboat Company in 1867 and then transferred to the Sassafras River Steamboat Company in 1878; later renamed *National Park* and ran on the Delaware River; abandoned 1906.

Commerce ON 4066, built 1864, Baltimore, Maryland; 188 gross tons, 100 horsepower; abandoned 1883. (NOTE: There were thirteen vessels named *Commerce* in the nineteenth century. This is the one believed to have operated on the Chester River.)

Corsica ON 126023, built 1881, Wilmington, Delaware; 145 feet long, 26 feet wide, 368 gross tons; built for Chester River Steamboat Company; sold to Maryland, Delaware and Virginia Railway in 1905; transferred to Baltimore, Chesapeake and Atlantic Railway in 1923; and sold to Long Island interests in 1923; operated on Long Island Sound until the 1930s and apparently was abandoned in 1938.

Emma A. Ford ON 135806, built 1884, Wilmington, Delaware; 180 feet long, 30 feet wide, 533 gross tons; built for Chester River Steamboat Company; acquired by the Maryland, Delaware and Virginia Railway in 1905; renamed *Love Point* in 1906; burned in 1906, rebuilt and burned a final time in 1909.

Emma Giles ON 135925, built 1887, Baltimore, Maryland; 549 gross tons, 178 feet long, 30 feet wide; converted to barge in 1939; abandoned 1952.

E.N. Fairchild ON 7907, built 1862, Ogdensburg, New York; 104 gross tons, 36 horsepower; abandoned 1879.

Endeavor ON 136531, built 1896, Philadelphia, Pennsylvania; 315 gross tons, 130 feet long, 23 feet wide; disposition unknown.

Enterprise operated on the Chester River by the Enterprise Transportation Company from about 1882 to about 1888. (NOTE: There were twenty-three vessels named *Enterprise* built between 1814 and 1867, and it is not clear which one was in service on the Chester.)

George Law ON 10044, built 1852; 147 feet long, 42 feet wide, 266 gross tons, 460 horsepower; sold by Chester River Steamboat Company in 1885 to undisclosed owner; burned at Bridgeton, New Jersey, on August 27, 1894.

Georgia ON 10039, built 1836, Baltimore, Maryland; 551 gross tons; chartered by U.S. War Department, 1863; abandoned 1878.

Gov. Wolcott, built 1825, New York; 131 gross tons; abandoned 1845. (NOTE: This vessel's name has appeared as both *Gov. Wolcott* and *Governor Wolcott*.)

Gratitude ON 85607, built 1880, Philadelphia, Pennsylvania; 133 feet long, 20 feet wide, 214 gross tons; renamed *Captain Miller* in 1882; burned April 23, 1887, in Centreville, Maryland; was rebuilt and again renamed *Gratitude* for the Centreville and Corsica River Steamboat Company; sunk in collision near Claiborne, Maryland, in 1914; was raised and sold to the Bennett Line for service out of Washington, D.C.; sold to Mateo Garcia of Havana, Cuba, in 1926; renamed *Cuba* and taken to the island nation, where her final disposition is unknown.

Hugh Jenkins ON 14013, built 1849, Baltimore, Maryland; 306 gross tons; sold to the U.S. Quartermaster Department on September 9, 1861; re-documented as *Kent Island* on March 8, 1866; abandoned 1877.

Isadore ON 12003, built 1864, Baltimore, Maryland; 127 gross tons; abandoned 1871.

Lauretta Curran ON 141707, built 1901, Madison, Maryland; 23 gross tons, 50 feet long, 23 feet wide. (NOTE: Gasoline engine powered.)

Maryland, built 1819, Baltimore, Maryland; 297 gross tons; operated on a variety of Chesapeake Bay routes; abandoned 1865.

Norfolk, built 1817, Norfolk, Virginia; 222 gross tons; abandoned 1840.

Osceola apparently operated in the Chesapeake Bay region, including the Chester River, from 1836 to 1888. (NOTE: Ten vessels with the name *Osceola* were listed in the *Lytle Holdcamper List*, making it difficult to determine which vessel ran on the Chester.)

Osiris, built 1838, New York, New York; 145 gross tons; came under the ownership of the Confederate States of America in 1861; final disposition is unknown.

Patuxent ON 5284, built 1827, Baltimore, Maryland; 219 gross tons; abandoned 1868.

Queen Anne ON 20621, built 1899, Baltimore, Maryland; 651 gross tons, 203 feet long, 52 feet wide; renamed *Rockaway;* abandoned 1930.

Queen Caroline ON 20637, built 1902, Baltimore, Maryland; 641 gross tons, 203 feet long, 52 feet wide; renamed *Montauk, Transford, Ramona* and *Richmond*; burned September 30, 1945, in Claremont, Virginia.

Sarah ON 122998, built 1855, Philadelphia, Pennsylvania; 196 gross tons; converted to a barge in 1890 and was used as such on the Chester River; disposition unknown.

Surprise, built 1817, Baltimore, Maryland; 92 gross tons; abandoned 1828.

Tourist ON 145859, built 1892, Nyack, New York; 284 gross tons, 116 feet long, 21 feet wide; final disposition unknown.

William Selden, built 1851, Washington, D.C.; 378 tons, 108 feet long, 25 feet wide; burned by retreating Confederate forces at the Norfolk, Virginia Navy Yard on May 10, 1862.

NOTES

CHAPTER 1

1. Rountree, Clark and Mountford, *John Smith's Chesapeake Voyages*, 118, 229.
2. Footner, *Rivers of the Eastern Shore*, 310.
3. Emory, *Queen Anne's County*, 395.
4. Burgess and Wood, *Steamboats*, xvii.
5. Ibid., xix.
6. Crawford, *Naval War of 1812*, 151, 152.
7. *Maryland Gazette and Political Intelligencer*, March 2, 1821.
8. Marestier, *Memoir on Steamboats*, 44.
9. Scharf, *History of Baltimore City*, 301.
10. Emory, *Queen Anne's County*, 17.
11. Marestier, *Memoir on Steamboats*, 38.

CHAPTER 2

12. Burgess and Wood, *Steamboats*, 12.
13. *Centreville Times and Eastern Shore Public Advertiser*, July 30, 1832.
14. Ibid., June 16, 1832.
15. *Kent News*, July 3, 1841.
16. Ibid., July 24, 1841.
17. Ibid.
18. Ibid., February 12, 1842.

19. Ibid., September 10, 1842.
20. Ibid.
21. Burgess and Wood, *Steamboats*, 12.
22. Emory, *Queen Anne's County*, 545.
23. *Centreville Times*, September 18, 1852.

CHAPTER 3

24. *Kent News*, May 7, 2009.
25. Ibid., October 28, 1865.
26. Ibid., date unknown.
27. Among the members of the Carmichael family who became well known were William Carmichael, who served with Benjamin Franklin in Paris during the American Revolution, and Judge Richard Bennett Carmichael, who was famously dragged from his Easton courtroom by Union troops and arrested for pro-Southern leanings.
28. Burgess, *Chesapeake Circle*, 51.
29. *Kent News*, April 13, 1861.
30. Ibid., April 23, 1864.
31. Ibid., March 28, 1863.
32. *Illustrated Atlas*.
33. *Kent News*, October 28, 1865.
34. Ibid.
35. *Sun*, October 28, 1865.
36. *Proceedings of the Maryland General Assembly*, 1866, vol. 107, 2049.
37. Ibid., 1867, chap. 24, 43.
38. *Chestertown Transcript*, May 15, 1869.

CHAPTER 4

39. *Laws of Maryland*, 1867, chap. 14, 14.
40. Ibid., 15.
41. *Kent News*, August 3, 1867.
42. Ibid.
43. *Chestertown Transcript*, May 15, 1869.
44. *Biographical Cyclopedia*.
45. Ibid.

46. *Kent News*, July 17, 1869.

47. Ibid., June 25, 1870.

48. *Sun*, February 29, 1872.

49. Ibid.

50. Ibid., October 11, 1875.

CHAPTER 5

51. *Kent News*, May 12, 1877.

52. Ibid., June 30, 1877.

53. *Chestertown Transcript*, July 6, 1877.

54. Brown, *Paddle Box Decorations*, 8.

55. *Chestertown Transcript*, July 6, 1877.

56. Usilton, *History of Kent County*, 116, 117.

57. *Biographical Cyclopedia*.

58. *Sun*, July 21, 1879.

59. *Kent News*, July 26, 1879.

60. *Minutes of the Board of Directors*, July 28, 1879.

61. Hall, *Baltimore*, 347.

62. Burgess and Wood, *Steamboats*, 58.

63. *Kent News*, May 10, 1884.

64. *Chestertown Transcript*, October 9, 1884.

65. Ibid.

CHAPTER 6

66. Byron, *Lord's Oysters*, 81.

67. *Sun*, June 17, 1956.

68. Footner, *Rivers of the Eastern Shore*, 324.

CHAPTER 7

69. Rhodes, *Queenstown*, 108.

70. Queen Anne's Railroad timetable, June 18, 1899.

71. *Centreville Observer*, February 2, 1899.

72. Ibid., date unknown.

73. Ibid., November 2, 1899.
74. *Sun*, October 28, 1899.
75. Burgess and Wood, *Steamboats*, 62.
76. *Centreville Observer*, December 21, 1899.
77. *Sun*, March 16, 1900.
78. Rhodes, *Queenstown*, 107.
79. *Sun*, August 20, 1900.
80. Ibid., May 14, 1902.
81. Ibid., February 23, 1904.

Chapter 8

82. Elliott, *Last of the Steamboats*, 5.
83. Ibid., 6.
84. Burgess and Wood, *Steamboats*, 212.
85. *Sun*, August 19, 1908.
86. Rhodes, *Queenstown*, 222.
87. Ibid., 110.
88. *Sun*, July 19, 1910.
89. There appears to be some uncertainty as to who built the Love Point Hotel and when. Is it the hotel the Queenstown and Love Point Transportation and Development Corporation planned? Various sources say it was built anywhere between 1890 and 1910, but there is no consensus.

Chapter 9

90. *New York Times*, July 4, 1861.
91. *Kent News*, July 13, 1861.
92. Latin Library, "Richard Thomas Zarvona."
93. Mills, *Chesapeake Bay*, 157.
94. Information provided by Kevin Hemstock, May 2015.
95. *Sun*, December 10, 1888.
96. Ibid.
97. *Centreville Observer*, March 2, 1899.
98. *Kent News*, January 17, 1903.
99. *Centreville Observer*, August 24, 1899.
100. Footner, *Rivers of the Eastern Shore*, 322.
101. *Kent News*, November 5, 1904.

Chapter 10

102. *Sun*, April 25, 1887.
103. Burgess and Wood, *Steamboats*, 59.
104. *Kent News*, December 10, 1887.
105. *Sun*, July 19, 1888.
106. *Report of the Chief of Engineers*, 1895.
107. *Kent News*, September 28, 1889.
108. Pfeiffer, Mid-Atlantic Regional Fruit Loop.
109. Ibid.
110. Hayman, *Rails Along the Chesapeake*, 59, 73.
111. Burgess and Wood, *Steamboats*, 63.
112. William Harry Hoyer, "The PRR's Navy, Part III," *The Keystone* 40, no. 4 (Winter 2007): 16–18.
113. *Centreville Observer*, August 26, 1896.
114. Ibid., December 21, 1899.
115. *Minutes of the Board of Directors*, April 17, 1902.
116. *Kent News*, October 15, 1904.
117. Baer and Orr, *Guide to Records*.
118. Hoyer, "The PRR's Navy, Part III," 25.
119. Baer and Orr, *Guide to Records*.
120. Burgess, *Chesapeake Circle*, 30–32.

Chapter 11

121. *Annual Reports of the Board of Directors of the Maryland, Delaware and Virginia Railway*, 1905 and 1906.
122. Ibid., 1908.
123. *Annual Report, Supervising General, U.S. Steamboat Inspector General*.
124. *Annual Reports of the Board of Directors of the Maryland, Delaware and Virginia Railway*, 1909–14.
125. *Centreville Observer*, April 25, 1914.
126. *Baltimore, Chesapeake and Atlantic Railway Company and Maryland, Delaware, and Virginia Railway Company Promotional Booklet*, 1915, 75.
127. Brown, *Steam Packets*, 86,87.
128. *Annual Reports of the Board of Directors of the Maryland, Delaware and Virginia Railway*, 1920.
129. Ibid.

130. *Centreville Observer*.
131. Information provided by Christopher W. Baer, January 2015.
132. *Kent News*, December 22, 1923.
133. Burgess, *Chesapeake Circle*, 34–36.
134. *Sun*, November 7, 1930.
135. Ibid., October 24, 1934.
136. *Chestertown Transcript*, June 13, 1936.
137 Holly, *Steamboat on the Chesapeake*, 136–37.
138. Ibid.
139. Usilton, *History of Kent County*, 251.

BIBLIOGRAPHY

BOOKS

Arnett, Earl, Robert J. Brugger and Edward C. Papenfuse. *Maryland: A New Guide to the Old Line State.* 2nd ed. Baltimore, MD: Johns Hopkins University Press, 1999.

Baer, Christopher T., and Craig A. Orr. *Guide to the Records of the Pennsylvania Railroad Company and Penn Central Transportation Company.* Vol. 5. Wilmington, DE: Hagley Museum, 2009.

The Biographical Cyclopedia of Representative Men of Maryland and the District of Columbia. Baltimore, MD: National Biographical Publishing Company, 1879.

Blanpied, Dave, and Eloise Blanpied. *Before the Refuge on Eastern Neck Island.* Chestertown, MD: Kent Printing Corporation, 2003.

Brown, Alexander Crosby. *Paddle Box Decorations of American Sound Steamboats.* Newport News, VA: Mariners Museum, 1943.

———. *Steam Packets on the Chesapeake.* Centreville, MD: Cornell Maritime Press, 1961.

Burgess, Robert H. *Chesapeake Circle.* Centreville, MD: Cornell Maritime Press, 1965.

———. *This Was Chesapeake Bay.* Centreville, MD: Cornell Maritime Press, 1963.

Burgess, Robert H., and H. Graham Wood. *Steamboats Out of Baltimore.* Centreville, MD: Tidewater Publishers, 1968.

Byron, Gilbert. *The Lord's Oysters.* Baltimore, MD: Johns Hopkins University Press, 1957.

Crawford, Michael J., ed. *The Naval War of 1812: A Documentary History*. Vol. 3, *1814–1815, Chesapeake Bay, Northern Lakes, and Pacific Ocean*. Washington, D.C.: Naval Historical Center, Department of the Navy, 2002.

Elliott, Richard V. *Last of the Steamboats: The Saga of the Wilson Line*. Centreville, MD: Tidewater Publishers, 1970.

Emory, Frederic. *Queen Anne's County, Maryland*. Queenstown, MD: Queen Anne Press, 1981.

Footner, Hulbert. *Rivers of the Eastern Shore*. Centreville, MD: Tidewater Publishers, 1944.

Hall, Clayton Coleman. *Baltimore: Its History and Its People*. Vol. 2. Baltimore, MD: Lewis Historical Publishing Company, 1912.

Hayman, John C. *Rails Along the Chesapeake: A History of Railroading on the Delmarva Peninsula 1827–1978*. N.p.: Marvadel Publishers, 1979.

Holly, David C. *Steamboat on the Chesapeake:* Emma Giles *and the Tolchester Line*. Centreville, MD: Tidewater Publishers, 1987.

Hoxter, Nick. *Growing Up on Kent Island*. Grasonville, MD: M.R.H. Publishing, LLC, 1996.

———. *A Walk Back in Time*. Grasonville, MD: M.R.H. Publishing, LLC, 1997.

Keatley, J.K. *Place Names of the Eastern Shore of Maryland*. Queenstown, MD: Queen Anne Press, 1987.

Kenny, Hamill. *The Place Names of Maryland: Their Origin and Meaning*. Baltimore: Maryland Historical Society, 1984.

Lewis, Brent. *Remembering Kent Island*. Charleston, SC: The History Press, 2009.

Lytle, William M., and Forrest R. Holdcamper. *The Lytle Holdcamper List*. Revised and edited by C. Bradford Mitchell. New York: Steamship Historical Society of America, Inc., 1975.

Marestier, Jean Baptiste. *Memoir on Steamboats of the United States of America*. Mystic, CT: Marine Historical Association, Inc., 1957.

Mills, Eric. *Chesapeake Bay in the Civil War*. Centreville, MD: Tidewater Publishers, 1996.

Plummer, Norman H. *Maryland's Oyster Navy: The First Fifty Years*. Chestertown, MD: Washington College, Literary House Press, 1993.

Rhodes, Harry C. *Queenstown: The Social History of a Small American Town*. Queenstown, MD: Queen Anne Press, 1985.

Rountree, Helen C., Wayne E. Clark and Kent Mountford. *John Smith's Chesapeake Voyages 1607–1609*. Charlottesville: University of Virginia Press, 2007.

Scharf, J. Thomas. *History of Baltimore City and County.* Baltimore, MD: Regional Publishing Company, 1971.

Sheads, Scott Sumpter, and Daniel Carroll Toomey. *Baltimore During the Civil War.* Linthicum, MD: Toomey Press, 1997.

Stanton, Samuel Ward. *New York Bay Steam Vessels.* Upper Montclair, NJ: H. Kneeland Whiting, 1966.

———. *Steam Vessels of Chesapeake and Delaware Bays and Rivers.* Upper Montclair, NJ: H. Kneeland Whiting, 1966.

U.S. Department of Commerce. *Merchant Vessels of the United States.* Washington, D.C.: U.S. Government Printing Office, various annual editions.

Usilton, Fred G. *History of Kent County, Maryland 1630–1916.* N.p.: privately published, 1916.

Wennersten, John R. *The Oyster Wars of Chesapeake Bay.* Centreville, MD: Tidewater Publishers, 1981.

Wood, Mary. *My Darling Alice.* Chestertown, MD: Indiantown Press, 1999.

Documents

Annual Reports of the Board of Directors of the Maryland, Delaware and Virginia Railway. Wilmington, Delaware, 1905–23. Hagley Museum, Wilmington, Delaware.

Annual Report, Supervising General, U.S. Steamboat Inspector General. Vol. 15, *Steamboat Inspection Service to the Secretary of Commerce and Labor.* Washington, D.C.: Government Printing Office, 1910, 319. Author's collection.

Baltimore, Chesapeake and Atlantic Railway and Maryland, Delaware and Virginia Railway Advertising Booklet. Baltimore, Maryland, circa 1915.

An Illustrated Atlas of Kent and Queen Anne's Counties. Philadelphia: Lake, Griffing and Stevenson, 1877.

Minutes of the Board of Directors of the Chester River Steamboat Company. Baltimore, Maryland, 1877–1905. Hagley Museum, Wilmington, Delaware.

Queen Anne's Railroad Company Timetable. A 1902 newspaper advertisement, author's collection.

Report of the Chief of Engineers, U.S. Army. Washington, D.C. 1895. Accessed via Google Books.

NEWSPAPERS

Centreville Observer, Centreville, MD.
Centreville Times and Eastern Shore Public Advertiser, Centreville, MD.
Centreville Times, Centreville, MD.
Chestertown Transcript, Chestertown, MD.
Kent News, Chestertown, MD.
Maryland Gazette and Political Intelligencer, Annapolis, MD.
New York Times, New York, NY.
Sun, Baltimore, MD.
Unidentified clippings in the author's collection.

PERIODICALS

The Keystone. Pennsylvania Railroad Technical and Historical Society.
Marine Engineering, 1877.

WEBSITES

The Latin Library. "Richard Thomas Zarvona (1833–1875)." From *Chesapeake Steamboats: Vanished Fleet*. by David C. Holly. Centreville, MD: Tidewater Publishers, 1994. http://www.thelatinlibrary.com/chron/civilwarnotes/zarvona.html.
Maryland State Archives. *Proceedings and Acts of the General Assembly, 1867*. Vol. 133, page 4226. January 17, 1867. Annapolis, Maryland. http://aomol.msa.maryland.gov/000001/000133/html/am133--4226.html.
———. *Proceedings and Acts of the General Assembly, 1867*. Vol. 133, page 4255. February 18, 1867. Annapolis, Maryland. http://aomol.msa.maryland.gov/000001/000133/html/am133--4255.html.
Pfeiffer, Douglas G. Mid-Atlantic Regional Fruit Loop: The Virginia Fruit Page; Extension, Research and Teaching in Fruit Crops. "Mid-Atlantic Stone Fruit, Teaching and Extension: Peach Yellows." Blacksburg: Department of Entomology, Virginia Tech, 2015. http:///www.virginiafruit.ento.vt.edu/peachyellows.html.
U.S. Naval War Records Office. *Official Records of the Union and Confederate Navies in the War of Rebellion*. Washington, D.C.: Government Printing Office. Online via Making of America, Cornell University Library. Series 1, vols. 1–27 and Series 2, vols. 1–3, 1894–1922. http://digital.library.cornell.edu/m/moawar/ofre.html.

INDEX

ABOUT THE AUTHOR

Jack Shaum is a veteran reporter who has worked in both print journalism and broadcast journalism. A native of Baltimore, he began his career as a reporter with the *News American* and then became press aide to Maryland congressman William O. Mills. Following that was a nearly thirty-year career as news anchor and reporter for news-talk radio station WBAL in Baltimore. He retired from that position in 2002 and is currently writing for the *Bay Times* and *Record Observer* newspapers in Queen Anne's County, Maryland.

He rode his first steamboat at the age of eight, a journey that started a lifelong love of steam-powered vessels. From 2002 to 2011, he was editor in chief of the quarterly journal of the Steamship Historical Society of America and wrote a number of articles for that publication. He was also its Mid-Atlantic columnist from 1975 to 2011. He is coauthor of *Majesty at Sea*, a history of the great four-funneled passenger liners, and co-ghost writer and coeditor of *Night Boat on the Potomac*, a history of the Norfolk and Washington Steamboat Company, written from the notes of the late Harry Jones. Other interests include Maryland history, the American Revolution, trains and model railroading.

For twenty years, he and his wife, Martha, traveled as lecturers on several East Coast cruise ships. They have two daughters and four grandchildren and live near Chestertown, Maryland.